TWO CELTIC SAINTS

THE LIVES OF
NINIAN AND KENTIGERN

TWO CELTIC SAINTS

THE LIFE OF
ST. NINIAN
by Ailred,

and

THE LIFE OF
ST. KENTIGERN
by Joceline.

Facsimile reprint 1989
by Llanerch Enterprises.
ISBN 0947992294.

PUBLISHER'S NOTE

This book contains translations from the Latin, of Ailred's Life of St. Ninian, and Joceline's Life of St. Kentigern. It has been reprinted from the series 'The Historians of Scotland' in a form to suit those who simply wish to read the lives of the two saints. Readers seeking more detailed background information, are referred to the volume in the Historians of Scotland, where they will find extensive notes of an academic nature, in English, but with numerous Latin quotations.

St. Ninian, from the fifth century, was the first apostle to the Picts; he seems to have been the first to build a stone church in these islands. His mission had limited success, and it was not until the late 6th., and early 7th., centuries that the Picts were converted by St. Columba, and the Britons of Strathclyde/Cumbria by St. Kentigern.

Both saints have associations with Glasgow. St. Ninian is said to have consecrated a cemetery there, implying the existence of an early monastic community, and St. Kentigern, by eventually selecting Glasgow as the seat of his bishopric, ensured the beginnings of a community that would grow into the modern city. Anecdotes in the life of St. Kentigern throw light on a little-known period of history, when Rhydderch was king of Alclyde, modern Dumbarton.

The drawing on the front cover shows an early inscribed cross from Whithorn which was found last century being used by a farmer as a gate-post. The spiral designs on the fly leaf and title page are from bosses on the cross of Nigg.

THE LIFE OF S. NINIAN

HERE BEGINNETH THE LIFE OF S. NINIAN, BISHOP AND CON-
FESSOR, BY AILRED, ABBOT OF RIEVAUX, TRANSLATED
FROM THE ANGLIC LANGUAGE INTO LATIN.[1]

PROLOGUE.

IT hath been the desire of many of the wise who
have lived before us to commit to writing the lives,
the manners, and the words of the saints, especially
of those who have flourished in their own times, and
thus to redeem from oblivion, and perpetuate the
memory of, the example of the more perfect life to the
edification of posterity. But they who had distinguished genius, and fluency of speech, and the lightness of eloquence, did this the more usefully in so far
as they gratified the ears of those who listened to
them by polished language. Yet those, to whom on
account of the barbarism of their native land, the
faculty of speaking gracefully and elegantly was lacking, did not defraud posterity of an account of those
who were to be imitated, although in a more simple
style. Hence it happened that a barbarous language
obscured the life of the most holy Ninian, whom the

---

[1] This is the superscription of the manuscript in the British Museum.

sanctity of his ways and his distinguished miracles
commend to us, and the less it gratified the reader
the less it edified him.   Accordingly it pleased thy
holy affection[1] to impose upon mine insignificance the
task of rescuing from a rustic style as from darkness,
and of bringing forth into the clear light of Latin
diction, the life of this most renowned man, a life
which had been told by those who came before me,
truly indeed, but in too barbarous a style.   I embrace
thy devotion, I approve thy desire, I praise thy zeal,
but I know mine own inexperience, and I fear to strip
it of the coarse garments in which it hath hitherto been
hidden, and not be able to deck it in those in which
it may appear more comely.   But since I cannot
refuse what thou dost enjoin, I will attempt what
thou commandest, as I prefer to be judged by thee
incompetent rather than obstinate.   Mayhap, what
my imperfection denieth, thy faith will supply, thy
prayer secure, thy sanctity obtain.   He too for whose
honour and love thou desirest me to do this will assist
thy pious vows, thine aspirations, and my attempt
and my study.   Moreover, by his merits, thou trustest
that to me may be given the learned tongue and the
copious speech.   To this must be added that which thou
sayest, that the clergy and people of thy holy church,
who are moved by a rare affection for the saint of God
under whose protection they live, will receive with
the greatest devotion what I write, since, as thou
sayest, the desires of all have specially selected me for

this work. I undertake therefore the burden which thou layest upon me, moved indeed by thy prayers, but quickened by faith. I will labour, as He will deign to aid me, who maketh eloquent the tongues of infants, so to temper my style, that on the one hand an offensive roughness obscure not so high a matter, and on the other hand, that a freedom of speech, not so eloquent as fatiguing, cheat not of the desired fruit of this my labour the simplicity of those who cannot appreciate a proper rhetoric. May the grace of the Saviour bless this undertaking, and may He who bestowed upon him the virtues whereby he is deemed meet to be held in everlasting remembrance make us who record them worthy, and bestow upon us the reward of our toil, that his prayer may ever attend us in the way whereby we hasten to our father-land. And in the hour of our departure, when we await the end of the way and the beginning of the life, may his consolation be near us, and for his holy merit's sake the eternal reward of the heavenly good things.

[THE PREFACE.

The Testimony of Bœda concerning Ninian, with observations of Ailred.]

DIVINE authority, which from the beginning is acknowledged to have constituted the holy patriarch Abraham a father of many nations, and a prince of the faith predestinated from ancient times, by such an oracle as this—" Get thee out of thy country, and from thy kindred, and from thy father's house, unto a land that I shall show thee, and I will make of thee a great nation,"[1] recommendeth to us the glorious life of the most holy Ninian, on this wise, that this most blessed one leaving his country, and his father's house, learnt in a foreign land that which afterwards he taught unto his own, "being placed by God over the nations and kingdoms, to root out, and to pull down, and to destroy, and to throw down, to build, and to plant."[2] Of this most holy man, Venerable Bæda, calling attention in a very few words to the sacred beginnings of his life, the tokens of his sanctity, the dignity of his office, the fruit of his ministry, his most excellent end, and the reward of his toil, thus writeth concerning him :—

" In the year after the incarnation of the Lord 565, at the time when Justin the Less, after Justinian, had received the government of the Roman Empire, there came to Britain out of Ireland a presbyter and abbot, remarkable for his monastic habit and rule, by name Columba, with the intention of preaching the word of God in the provinces of the Northern Picts; that is, to those who were separated from the southern regions by lofty and rugged ranges of mountains. For the Southern Picts themselves, who dwell on this side of the same mountains, had long before abandoned idolatry, and embraced the faith in the truth, by the preaching of the word by Bishop Ninian, a most reverend and holy man, of the nation of the Britons, who had at Rome been regularly instructed in the faith and mysteries of the truth; the seat of whose episcopate, dedicated to S. Martin, and a remarkable church, where he resteth in the body along with many saints, the nation of the Angles now possesseth. That place, appertaining to the province of the Bernicii, is vulgarly called 'At the White House,' for that there he built a church of stone in a way unusual among the Britons."

On the trustworthy testimony of this great author, we have been made acquainted with the origin of S. Ninian, in that he stateth that he was of the race of the Britons, trained in the rules of the faith in the Holy Roman Church; with his office, in that he declareth him to have been a bishop and a preacher of the word of God; with the fruit of his labours, in that he proveth that the Southern Picts were converted from idolatry to the true religion by his toil; and, with his end, in that he witnesseth that he resteth along with many saints in the Church of S. Martin. But that which he briefly, in view of the tenor of his history, seemeth barely to have touched upon, a book of his Life and Miracles, written in a barbarous style detaileth at greater length. This book, never varying from the foundation of this witness, hath recorded in historical fashion the way whereby he made this commencement, merited such fruit, and attained unto so worthy an end.

[CHAPTER I.

The Birth of Ninian, and his Training.]

THEREFORE in the island of Britannia, which long ago, as they say, took its name from Brutus, among a race of the same name, and of no ignoble family, did the blessed Ninian spring: in that region, it is supposed, in the western part of the island (where the ocean stretching as an arm, and making as it were on either side two angles, divideth at this day the realms of the Scots and the Angles), which till these last times belonging to the Angles, is proved not only by historical record but by actual memory of individuals to have had a king of its own. His father was a king, by religion a Christian, of such faith in God, and of such merit, as to be deemed worthy of a child by whom what was lacking to the faith of his own nation was supplied, and by whom another race that had not known the sacraments of the faith became imbued with the mysteries of our holy religion. He in very infancy, regenerated in the water of holy baptism, preserving immaculate the nuptial robe which clad in white he had received, a conqueror of vice, presented it in the sight of Christ; and that Holy Spirit whom he first received to cleanse him, he merited by his most holy ways to maintain as the instructor of his pious heart. For by His guidance, while yet a boy, though not in sense one, he shunned whatsoever was contrary to religion, adverse to chastity, opposed to good morals, and discordant with the laws of the truth. But whatsoever was of the law, of grace, of good report, whatsoever was useful to man, or well-pleasing to God, that he ceased not to follow with a mind already mature. Happy was he whose delight was in the law of the Lord day and night, who like a tree planted by the water-side brought forth his fruit in due season, seeing that in the vigour of manhood he strenuously fulfilled that which he had learnt with the greatest devotion. Wonderful was his reverence about churches; great his love for the brethren. He was sparing in food, reticent in speech, assiduous in study, agreeable in manners, averse from jesting, and in everything subjecting the flesh to the spirit. Wherefore bending his mind to the sacred Scriptures, when he had learnt according to their way the rules of the faith from the more learned of his race, the young man came by the exercise of his penetrating genius to see, what by the divine inspiration he had gathered from the Scriptures, that much was wanting to their perfection. On this his mind began to be agitated, and not enduring anything short of perfection, he toiled and sighed. His heart was hot within him, and at last in meditation the fire kindled. "And what," said he, "shall I do? I have sought in mine own land Him whom my soul loveth. I sought Him, but I have found Him not. I will arise now, and I will compass sea and land. I will seek the truth which my soul loveth. Surely needeth it such toil as this. Was it not said to Peter, 'Thou art Peter, and on this rock I will build my church; and the gates of hell shall not prevail against it'? Therefore in the faith of Peter there is naught inferior, naught obscure, naught imperfect, naught against which false doctrine and perverse opinions, like the gates of hell, can prevail. And where is the faith of Peter but in the See of Peter? Thither certainly, thither I must betake me, that, going forth from my land, and from my kinsfolk, and from the house of my father, I may be deemed meet in the land of vision to behold the fair beauty of the Lord, and to visit His temple. The false prosperity of the age smileth on me, the

vanity of the world allureth me, the love of earthly relation-
ship softeneth my soul, toil and the weariness of the flesh
deter me, but the Lord hath said, 'He that loveth father or
mother more than me is unworthy of me, and he that taketh
not up his cross and followeth me is unworthy of me.' I have
learnt moreover that they who despise the royal court shall
attain to the heavenly kingdom." Wherefore, animated by the
impulse of the Holy Spirit, spurning riches, and treading
down all earthly affections, the noble youth betook himself to
pilgrimage, and having crossed the Britannic sea, and entered
Italy by the Gallican Alps, he safely arrived at the city.

[CHAPTER II.

He arriveth at Rome—He is consecrated Bishop by the Pope—
His Intercourse with S. Martin—His Return unto his
Native Land.]

THE most blessed youth having arrived at Rome, when he
had shed tears, proofs of his devotion, before the sacred relics
of the apostles, and had with many prayers commended the
desire of his heart to their patronage, betook himself to the
Bishop of the Supreme See, and when he had explained to
him the cause of his journey, the Pope accepted his devotion,
and treated him with the greatest affection as his son. Presently he handed him over to the teachers of truth to be imbued
with the disciplines of faith and the sound meanings of Scripture. But the young man, full of God, took notice that he had
not laboured in vain or to no purpose; he learnt moreover that
on him and his fellow-countrymen many things contrary to
sound doctrine had been inculcated by unskilled teachers.
Therefore with the greatest eagerness, with enlarged mouth,
receiving the word of God, like a bee he formed for himself
the honeycombs of wisdom by arguments from the different
opinions of doctors, as of various kinds of flowers. And
hiding them within his inmost heart, he preserved them to
be inwardly digested and brought forward for the refreshment
of his inward man and for the consolation of many others.
Verily it was a worthy recompense that he who for the love
of truth had despised country, wealth, and delights—brought,
if I may so say, into the secret chambers of truth, and admitted
to the very treasures of wisdom and knowledge,—should re-

ceive for carnal things spiritual things, for earthly things
heavenly things, for temporal blessings eternal goods. Meanwhile, as chaste in body, prudent in mind, provident in
counsel, circumspect in every act and word, he was in the
mouths of all, it happened that he rose to the favour and
friendship of the Supreme Pontiff himself. Wherefore, after
living in a praiseworthy manner for many years in the city,
and having been sufficiently instructed in the sacred Scriptures,
he attained to the height of virtue, and, sustained on the wings
of love, he rose to the contemplation of spiritual things. Then
the Roman Pontiff, hearing that some in the western parts of
Britain had not yet received the faith of our Saviour, and that
some had heard the word of the gospel either from heretics or
from men ill instructed in the law of God, moved by the Spirit
of God, consecrated the said man of God to the episcopate with
his own hands, and, after giving him his benediction, sent him
forth as an apostle to the people aforesaid. There flourished at
this time the most blessed Martin, Bishop of the city of Tours,
whose life, rendered glorious by miracles, already described by
the most learned and holy Sulpicius, had enlightened the whole
world. Therefore the man of God, returning from the City, full
of the Spirit of God, and touched with the desire of seeing him,
turned aside to the city of Tours. With what joy, devotion,
and affection he was received by him, who shall easily tell?
By the grace of prophetic illumination the worth of the new
bishop was not hid from him, whom by revelation he recognised
as sanctified by the Holy Spirit and sure to be profitable to
the salvation of many. The pillars in the tabernacle of God
are joined one with the other, and two cherubim stretching
out their wings touch each other; sometimes borne up on the
wings of virtue they soar to God, sometimes standing and fold-
ing their wings they become edifying to each other. Therefore
coming back from these exalted things to what is earthly,
blessed Ninian besought of the saint masons, stating that he
proposed to himself that, as in faith, so in the ways of building
churches and in constituting ecclesiastical offices, he desired
to imitate the holy Roman Church. The most blessed man
assented to his wishes; and so, satiated with mutual conversa-
tions as with heavenly feasts, after embraces, kisses, and tears,
shed by both, they parted, holy Martin remaining in his own
See, and Ninian hastening forth under the guidance of Christ
to the work whereunto the Holy Ghost had called him. Upon
his return to his own land a great multitude of the people

went out to meet him; there was great joy among all, and wonderful devotion, and the praise of Christ sounded out on all sides, for they held him for a prophet. Straightway that active husbandman of the Lord proceeded to root up what had been ill planted, to scatter what had been ill gathered, to cast down what had been ill built. Having purged the minds of the faithful from all their errors, he began to lay in them the foundations of faith unfeigned; building thereon the gold of wisdom, the silver of knowledge, and the stones of good works: and all the things to be done by the faithful he both taught by word and illustrated by example, confirming it by many and great signs following.

[CHAPTER III.

The Foundation of the Church of Whithern.]

BUT he selected for himself a site in the place which is now termed Witerna, which, situated on the shore of the ocean, and extending far into the sea on the east, west, and south sides, is closed in by the sea itself, while only on the north is a way open to those who would enter. There, therefore, by the command of the man of God, the masons whom he had brought with him built a church, and they say that before that none in Britannia had been constructed of stone. And having first learnt that the most holy Martin, whom he held always in wondrous affection, had passed from earth to heaven, he was careful to dedicate the church itself in his honour.

[CHAPTER IV.

He healeth and converteth King Tuduvallus.]

THEREFORE this light set upon a candlestick began to those who were in the house of the Lord to shine forth in heavenly signs and radiant flames of virtue, and to enlighten darkened minds with the clear and burning word of the Lord, and to warm the cold. There was in that region a king (for the whole island lay subjected to diverse kings), by name Tuduvallus, whom riches, power, and honour had excited to pride, in whom the lust of the flesh, and the lust of the eye, and the wealth of the world had so ministered to his haughtiness, that he presumed himself to be able to do as much as any one, and he had the presumption to believe that what any one could do was both possible and lawful to him also. He, despising the admonitions of the man of God, alike secretly depreciated his doctrine and manners, and openly opposed his sound teaching, so that the earth seemed rejected and nigh to cursing, in that, drinking in the rain that came oft upon it, it brought forth thorns and thistles, and not wholesome herbs. But at a certain time, when he had been more than usually hostile to the man of God, the heavenly Judge suffered no longer that the injury to his servant should go unavenged, but struck him on the head with an unbearable disease, and broke the crown of the head of him that walked in his sins. To such an extent did his sickness prevail that a sudden blindness darkened those haughty eyes, and he who had opposed the light of truth lost the light of sense; but not in vain, nor to the increase of his folly. For the poor man lay oppressed by pain, deprived of sight; but, darkened externally, he became enlightened in the inward parts. When returning unto himself he confessed his sin, seeking a remedy from him alone, to whom he had hitherto exhibited himself as an enemy. At last, calling together his relations, taking advice from them, since he could not go himself, being debarred by his infirmity, he sent messengers to the man of God, beseeching him not to enter into judgment with his servant, nor to reward him according to his deeds, but as an imitator of the divine benignity, to return good for evil, love for hatred. The most blessed man hearing this, not elated with human pride, but abounding as ever in the bowels of compassion, having first offered up prayer to God, went straightway to the sick man with the greatest kindness and devotion. And first he corrected him with tender reproof, and then touching the head of the sick man with healing hand, he signed the blind eyes with the sign of the saving life. What shall I more say? The pain fled, the blindness was driven away by the coming light, and so it came to pass that the disease of the body cured the disease of the soul, and the power of the man of God expelled the disease of the body. Healed therefore in both, in body and mind, he began thenceforth with all affection to cherish and venerate the saint of God, knowing by experience that the Lord was with him, and directed all his ways, giving him power against everything that exalteth itself against the knowledge of Christ, since He was ready to avenge every disobedience and injury inflicted on the servants of Christ.

If, therefore, this contemptuous and proud man, by the grace
of humiliation and penance, was deemed meet to be healed
by the holy man, who shall doubt that he, who with sure faith
and sincere and humble heart, seeks the aid of so great a saint
for the curing the wounds of his inner man, shall obtain a
speedy remedy by his holy merits. But let us now go on to
other things, which seem so much the greater, in proportion as
they are proved to be contrary to nature itself.

[CHAPTER V.

He cleareth the Presbyter accused of Violation.]

THERE was a certain girl in the service of one of the noble-
men, as to the sinful flesh fair of face and graceful of aspect,
on whom, when an unchaste young man had cast his eyes,
he was seized with a blind love, and not able to subdue the
flame of the lust which he had conceived, began to urge the
girl to consent to sin. At length by solicitation or by money,
he caused that she should conceive sorrow to bring forth
iniquity. The unhappy woman yielded to the other's lust, little
recking of the judgment of God, while she hoped to evade the
eyes of man; but by the swelling of her womb the crime was
betrayed, and soon laughter was turned into weeping, joy into
sorrow, pleasure into pain. But what could she do? whither
turn? The law, her parent, her master were feared. Wherefore the unhappy woman made a covenant with death, and put
her trust in a lie, believing that she would seem less guilty if
she said that she had been deceived or forced by some one of
great name. Being urged therefore by the elders to denounce
the guilty man, she laid the charge of violence on the presbyter
to whom the bishop had delegated the care of the parish. All
were astonished who heard that word. They acquitted the girl
of the crime which they thought a man of such authority had
committed. The good were scandalized, the wicked elated, the
common people laughed, and the sacred order was scoffed at;
the presbyter, whose fame was injured, was saddened. But the
innocence of the priest by the revelation of the Spirit was not
hidden from the bishop beloved by God. He bore, however,
with impatience the scandal to the Church and the injury to
holy religion. Meanwhile the days of the woman were accomplished that she should bring forth a child, and she bore a son,
not, as was supposed, to the disgrace of the priest, but to that
of the father and the unworthy mother. For the bishop sum-

moned to the Church all the clergy and people, and having
exhorted them in a sermon, laid his hands on those who had
been baptized. Meanwhile the bold woman, casting aside all
shame, bursting in among the people with those who belonged
to her, thrust the child in the face of the presbyter, and vocife-
rated in the ears of all the congregation that he was the father
of the child, a violator and deceiver. A clamour arose among
the people; shame among the good, laughter among the wicked.
But the saint, commanding the people to keep quiet, ordered
the child to be brought to him, being then only one night old.
Wherefore, inflamed by the Spirit of God, when he had fixed his
eyes on him, he said, " Hearken, O child, in the name of Jesus
Christ, say out before this people if this presbyter begat thee."
O this marvel! O work worthy of all admiration! O the
strange clemency of God! O the ineffable power of the faith
of Christ! Verily, all things are possible to him that believeth;
but what shall I say ? [What could not the faith of Ninian
do? Certainly nature waiteth on faith, age on virtue; shall not
nature wait upon the Lord of Nature ?] Age is not needed to
produce an instrument, nor teaching for the office, nor time for
practice, but at the instance of faith the divine power gave
eloquence to the tongue of the infant, and out of the mouth
of a babe and suckling, it confounded the guilty, convicted the
liar, absolved the innocent. Accordingly out of the infant
body a manly voice was heard; the untaught tongue formed
rational words. Stretching out his hand, and pointing out his
real father among the people,—"This," said he, " is my father.
He begat me. He committed the crime laid upon the priest.
Verily, O bishop, thy priest is innocent of this guilt, and there
is naught between him and me but the community of the same
nature." This was enough. The child thereupon became
silent, to speak again by and bye according to the law of nature
and the changes of advancing years. Thanksgiving sounded
in the mouth of all, and the voice of praise, and all the people
exulted with joy, understanding that a great prophet had risen
among them, and that God had visited His people.

[CHAPTER VI.

He undertaketh the Conversion of the Picts—He returneth home.]

MEANWHILE the most blessed man, being pained that the
devil, driven forth from the earth within the ocean, should find

rest for himself in a corner of this island in the hearts of the Picts, girded himself as a strong wrestler to cast out his tyranny; taking, moreover, the shield of faith, the helmet of salvation, the breastplate of charity, and the sword of the Spirit, which is the word of God. Fortified by such arms, and surrounded by the society of his holy brethren as by a heavenly host, he invaded the empire of the strong man armed, with the purpose of rescuing from his power innumerable victims of his captivity: wherefore, attacking the Southern Picts, whom still the Gentile error which clung to them induced to reverence and worship deaf and dumb idols, he taught them the truth of the gospel and the purity of the Christian faith, God working with him, and confirming the word with signs following. The blind see, the lame walk, the lepers are cleansed, the deaf hear, the dead are raised, those oppressed of the devil are set free. A door is opened for the Word of God by the grace of the Holy Spirit; the faith is received, error renounced, temples cast down, churches erected. To the font of the saving laver run rich and poor, young and old, young men and maidens, mothers with their children, and, renouncing Satan with all his works and pomps, they are joined to the body of the believers by faith, by confession, and by the sacraments. They give thanks to the most merciful God, who had revealed His Name in the islands that are afar off, sending to them a preacher of truth, the lamp of their salvation, calling them His people which were not His people, and them beloved which were not beloved, and them as having found mercy who had not found mercy. Then the holy bishop began to ordain presbyters, consecrate bishops, distribute the other dignities of the ecclesiastical ranks, and divide the whole land into certain parishes. Finally, having confirmed the sons whom he had begotten in Christ in faith and good works, and having set in order all things that referred to the honour of God and the welfare of souls, bidding his brethren farewell, he returned to his own church, where, in great tranquillity of soul, he spent a life perfect in all sanctity and glorious for miracles.

[CHAPTER VII.

The Miracle among the Leeks.]

IT happened on a day that the holy man with his brethren entered the refectory to dine, and seeing no pot-herbs or vegetables on the table, he called the brother to whom the care of the garden had been committed, and asked the reason why upon that day no leeks or herbs had been placed before the brethren. Then he said, " Verily, O father, whatever remained of the leeks and such like I this day committed to the ground, and the garden has not yet produced anything fit for eating." Then said the saint, " Go, and whatsoever thy hand findeth, gather and bring to me." Wondering, he stood trembling, hesitating what to do; but knowing that Ninian could order nothing in vain, he slowly entered the garden. Then followed a wonder, incredible to all save those who knew that to him that believeth all things are possible. He beheld leeks and other kinds of herbs not only grown, but bearing seed. He was astonished, and, as if in a trance, thought that he saw a vision. Finally, returning to himself, and calling to mind the power of the holy man, he gave thanks unto God, and culling as much as seemed sufficient, placed it on the table before the bishop. The guests looked at each other, and with heart and voice magnified God working in His saints; and so retired much better refreshed in mind than in body.

[CHAPTER VIII.

Of the Animals and the Thieves.]

IT sometimes pleased the most holy Ninian to visit his flocks and the huts of his shepherds, wishing that the flocks, which he had gathered together for the use of the brethren, the poor and the pilgrims, should be partakers of the episcopal blessing. Therefore, all the animals being gathered into one place, when the servant of the Lord had looked upon them, he lifted up his hand and commended all that he had to the Divine protection. Going, therefore, round them all, and drawing as it were a little circle with the staff on which he leant, he enclosed the cattle, commanding that all within that space should that night remain under the protection of God. Having done all this, the man of God turned aside to rest for the night at the house of a certain honourable matron. When, after refreshing their bodies with food and their minds with the word of God, all had gone to sleep, certain thieves appeared, and seeing that the cattle were neither enclosed by walls, nor protected by hedges, nor kept in by a ditch, they looked to see if any one was watching, or if anything else resisted their attempt. And when they saw that all was silent, and that nothing was present that by voice or movement or barking might frighten them, they rushed in and crossed the bounds which the saint had fixed for the cattle, wishing to carry them all off. But the Divine power was present resisting the ungodly, nay, casting them down, using against those, who, as brute beasts, minded their bellies and not their reason, the instrumentality of an irrational animal. For the bull of the herd rushed upon the men in fury, and striking at the leader of the thieves, threw him down, pierced his belly with his horns, sending forth his life and his entrails together. Then tearing up the earth with his hoofs, he smote with mighty strength a stone which happened to be under his foot, and, in a wonderful way, in testimony of the miracle, the foot sunk into it as if into soft wax, leaving a footmark in the rock, and by the footmark giving a name to the place. For to this day the place in the English tongue is named Farres Last, that is, the Footprint of the Bull. Meanwhile, the most blessed father having finished the solemn service of prayer, went aside, and finding the man disembowelled and lying dead among the feet of the cattle, and seeing the others rushing about hither and thither as if possessed by furies, moved with compassion, and turning earnestly to God, besought Him to raise the dead. Nor did he cease from tears and entreaties till the same power which had slain him restored him not merely to life, but made him safe and sound. For, verily, the power of Christ, for the merit of the saint, smote him and healed him, killed and restored him to life, cast him down to hell and raised him again. Meanwhile the others, whom, running about the whole night, a certain madness had enclosed within the circle which the saint had made, seeing the servant of God, cast themselves with fear and trembling at his knees imploring pardon. And he, benignantly chiding them and impressing upon them the fear of God and the judgment prepared for the rapacious, giving them his benediction, granted them permission to depart.

[CHAPTER IX.

Ailred complaineth of the Morals of his own Age—Ninian's way of Life—The Miracle of the Shower.]

As I reflect on the devout conversation of this most holy man, I am ashamed of our sloth, and of the laziness of this miserable generation. Which of us, I ask, even among servants, does not more frequently utter jestings than things serious, idle things than things useful, carnal things rather than things spiritual, in common conversation and intercourse? The mouths that Divine grace consecrated for the praise of God, and for the celebration of the holy mysteries, are daily polluted by backbiting and secular words, and they weary of the Psalms, the Gospel, and the Prophets. They all the day busy themselves with the vain and base works of man. How do they conduct themselves when journeying? Is not the body like the mind, all day in motion while the tongue is idle? Rumours and the doings of wicked men are in men's mouths; religious gravity is relaxed by mirth and idle tales; the affairs of kings, the duties of bishops, the ministries of clerics, the quarrels of princes, above all, the lives and morals of all are discussed. We judge every one but ourselves, and, what is more to be deplored, we bite and devour one another, that we may be consumed one of another.[1] Not so the most blessed Ninian, not so, whose repose no crowd disturbed, whose meditation no journey hindered, whose prayer never grew lukewarm through fatigue. For whithersoever he went forth, he raised his soul to heavenly things, either by prayer or by contemplation. But so often as turning aside from his journey he indulged in rest, either for himself or for the beast on which he rode, bringing out a book which he carried about with him for the very purpose, he delighted in reading or singing something, for he felt with the prophet, "O how sweet are thy words unto my throat! yea, sweeter than honey unto my mouth."[2] Whence the Divine power bestowed such grace upon him, that even when resting in the open air, when reading in the heaviest rain, no moisture ever touched the book on which he was intent. When all around him was everywhere wet with water running upon it, he alone sat with his little book under the waters, as if he were protected by the roof of a house. Now it happened that the most reverend man was making a journey

with one of his brethren then alive, also a most holy person, by
name Plebia, and as his custom was he solaced the weariness
of his journey with the Psalms of David. And when, after a
certain portion of the journey, they turned aside from the
public road, that they might rest a little, having opened their
Psalters, they proceeded to refresh their souls with sacred reading. Presently the pleasant serenity of the weather, becoming
obscured by black clouds, poured down from on high to earth
those waters which it had naturally drawn upwards. What
shall I more say? The light air, like a chamber arching itself
around the servants of God, resisted as an impenetrable wall
the descending waters. But during the singing, the most
blessed Ninian turned off his eyes from the book, affected a
little by an unlawful thought, even with some desire he was
tickled by a suggestion of the devil. Whereupon at once the
shower, invading him and his book, betrayed what was hidden.
Then the brother, who was sitting by him, knowing what had
taken place, with gentle reproof reminded him of his order and
age, and showed him how unbecoming such things were in
such as he. Straightway the man of God, coming to himself,
blushed that he had been overtaken by a vain thought, and in
the same moment of time drove away the thought and stayed
the shower.

[CHAPTER X.

The Miracles of the Staff of Ninian in the Sea and on Land.]

MEANWHILE many, both nobles and men of the middle rank,
intrusted their sons to the blessed Pontiff to be trained in
sacred learning. He indoctrinated these by his knowledge,
he formed them by his example, curbing by a salutary discipline the vices to which their age was prone, and persuasively
inculcating the virtues whereby they might live soberly, righteously, and piously. Once upon a time one of these young
men committed a fault which could not escape the saint, and
because it was not right that discipline should be withheld from
the offender, the rods, the severest torments of boys, were made
ready. The lad in terror fled, but not being ignorant of the
power of the holy man, was careful to carry away with him the
staff on which he used to lean, thinking that he had procured
the best comfort for the journey, if he took with him anything

that belonged to the saint. Flying therefore from the face of the man, he sought diligently for a ship which might transport him to Scocia. It is the custom in that neighbourhood to frame of twigs a certain vessel in the form of a cup, of such a size that it can contain three men sitting close together. By stretching an ox-hide over it, they render it not only buoyant, but actually impenetrable by the water. Possibly at that time vessels of immense size were built in the same way. The young man stumbled on one of these lying at the shore, but not covered with leather, into which, when he had incautiously entered, by Divine providence, I know not whether by its natural lightness (for on a slight touch these float far out into the waves), straightway the ship was carried out to sea. As the water poured in, the unhappy sailor stood in ignorance what he should do, whither he should turn, what course he should pursue. If he abandon the vessel, his life is in danger; certain death awaiteth him if he continue. Then at length the unhappy boy, repenting his flight, beheld with pale countenance the waves ready to avenge the injury done to the father. At length, coming to himself, and thinking that S. Ninian was present in his staff, he confessed his fault, as if in his presence, in a lamentable voice, besought pardon, and prayed that by his most holy merits the divine aid might be vouchsafed him. Then trusting in the known kindness as well as power of the bishop, he stuck the staff in one of the holes, that posterity might not be ignorant of what Ninian could do even on the sea. At once, at the touch of the staff, the element trembled, and, as if kept back by a divine influence, ventured not to enter further by the open holes. These are Thy works, O Christ, who speaking to Thy disciples, hast endowed Thy faithful ones with this promise—"He that believeth in me, the works that I do, he shall do also." Thou didst imprint Thy sacred Footsteps on the waves of the sea: the power of Ninian controlled the natural power of the sea. Thy sacred Hand held up the doubting disciple on that account in danger among the waves: the staff of Ninian protected the fugitive disciple from being swallowed up by the billows. Thou didst command the winds and the waves, that the fear of Thy disciples might be dispelled: the power of Ninian subdued the winds and the sea, that the young man might reach safely the shore where he would be.

For a wind rising from the easterly quarter impelled the vessel gently. The staff, acting for sail, caught the wind; the staff as helm directed the vessel; the staff as anchor stayed it. The people stand on the western shore, and seeing a little vessel like a bird resting on the waters, neither propelled by sail, nor moved by oar, nor guided by helm, wondered what this miracle might mean. Meanwhile the young man landed, and that he might make the merits of the man of God more widely known, animated by faith he planted his staff on the shore, praying God, that in testimony of so great a miracle, sending forth roots and receiving sap contrary to nature, it might produce branches and leaves, and bring forth flowers and fruit. The divine propitiousness was not wanting to the prayer of the suppliant, and straightway the dry wood, sending forth roots, covering itself with new bark, put forth leaves and branches, and, growing into a considerable tree, made known the power of Ninian to the beholders there. Miracle is added to miracle. At the root of the tree a most limpid fountain springing up, sent forth a crystal stream, winding along with gentle murmur, with lengthened course, delightful to the eye, sweet to the taste, and useful and health-giving to the sick, for the merits of the saint.

[CHAPTER XI.

Declamation on the Death of Ninian—His Burial at Whithern.]

WHEREFORE the most blessed Ninian, wondrously shining with such miracles as these, and powerful in the highest virtues, advanced with prosperous course to the day of his summons. That day was a day of exultation and joy to the blessed man, but of tribulation and misery to the people. He rejoiced, to whom heaven was opened; the people mourned, who were bereaved of such a father. He rejoiced, for whom an eternal crown was laid up; they were in sorrow, whose salvation was endangered. But even his own joy was dashed with sorrow, since both leaving them seemed heavy to bear, yet to be longer separate from Christ intolerable. But Christ, thus consoling the hesitating soul, said, " Arise, hasten, my friend, my dove, and come. Arise," saith He, "my friend, arise, my dove, arise through the mind, hasten by desire, come by love." Verily this word suited the most holy man, as the friend of the Bridegroom, to whom that heavenly Bridegroom had consigned His bride; to whom He had revealed His secrets ; to whom He had opened His treasures. Rightly was that soul termed friend to whom all was love, nothing fear. He saith, my friend, my dove. O dove, verily taught to mourn, who, ignorant of the gall of bitterness, used to weep with those that wept, to be weak with the weak, to burn with those that are offended. Arise, hasten, my friend, my dove, and come; for the winter is now past, the rain is over and gone. Then verily, O blessed man, the winter was past to thee, when thou wert deemed meet with joyful eye to contemplate that heavenly fatherland, which the Sun of Righteousness doth illumine with the light of His glory, which love enkindleth, which a wondrous calm, as of a genial spring-time, tempereth with an unspeakable uniformity of climate. Then to thee that wintry storm which unsettleth all things here below, which hardeneth the cold hearts of men by the inroads of vice, in which neither doth the truth shine fully nor doth charity burn, hath passed away, and the showers of temptation and the hailstorms of persecution have ceased. That holy soul, perfectly triumphant, hath departed into the glory of perpetual freshness. The flowers, saith he, appear on the earth. The celestial odour of the flowers of paradise breathed upon thee, O blessed Ninian, when the company of the martyrs clad in red, and the confessors clothed in white, with placid countenance, smiled on thee as their most familiar friend, and welcomed to their society, thee, whom chastity had made white, and love had made red as the rose. For although opportunity granted not the sign of actual martyrdom in the body, it denied him not that merit of martyrdom, without which martyrdom is nothing. For how often did he for righteousness' sake expose himself to the sword of the enemy, how often to the arms of tyrants, prepared to lay down his life for truth, to die for righteousness? Rightly therefore to the flowers of the roses and the lilies of the valleys is this empurpled and radiant one summoned, ascending from Libanus, that he may be crowned among the hosts of heaven. For the time of engrafting had come; for the ripened cluster was to be cut off from the stem of the body, or from the vineyard of the Church here below, to be melted by love and laid up in the heavenly cellars.

Wherefore blessed Ninian, perfect in life and full of years, passed from this world in happiness, and was carried into heaven, accompanied by the angelic spirits, to receive an eternal reward, where, associated with the company of the apostles, joined to the ranks of the martyrs, enlisted in the hosts of the holy confessors, adorned also with the flowers of the virgins, he faileth not to succour those who hope in him, who cry to him, who praise him. But he was buried in the Church of Blessed Martin, which he had built from the foundations, and he was placed in a stone sarcophagus near the altar, the clergy and people present, with their voices and hearts sounding forth celestial hymns, to the accompaniment of sighs and tears; where the power which had shone in the living saint ceaseth not to make itself manifest about the body of the departed one, that all the faithful may acknowledge that he is dwelling in heaven, who ceaseth not to work on earth. For at his most sacred tomb the sick are cured, the lepers are cleansed, the wicked are terrified, the blind receive their sight; by all which things the faith of believers is confirmed, to the praise and glory of our Lord Jesus Christ, who liveth and reigneth with God the Father in the unity of the Holy Ghost, world without end. Amen.

[CHAPTER XII.

Miracles of the Relics of Ninian.]

(1. *In a deformed poor man.*)

WHEREFORE when the most blessed Ninian had been translated into the heavens, the faithful people who had loved him in life, frequented with the greatest devotion that which seemed to them to be left of him, namely, his most sacred relics; and the Divine Power, approving this reverence and faith, gave evidence by frequent miracles that he whom the common lot had removed from earth was living in heaven. There was born to one of the people by his own wife, a wretched son, the grief of both his parents, the horror of those who beheld him, whom nature had formed contrary to nature, all his members being turned the wrong way. For the joints of his feet being twisted, his heels projected forward, his back adhered to his face, his breast was near the hinder part of his head, with twisted arms his hands rested on his elbows. What more shall I say? There lay that dusky figure, to whom had been given useless members, a fruitless life, to whom, amid the wreck of his other members, the tongue alone remained to bewail his misery, and to move to tears and sorrow those who beheld and heard him. The sorrow of his parents was incessant. Their grief increased day by day. At length the power of the most blessed Ninian, so often experienced, came into their minds, and, full of faith, they take up that wretched body, and approaching the relics of the holy man, they offer the sacrifice of a contrite heart with floods of tears, and continue instant in devout prayer till the hour of vespers. Then laying that unshapely form before the tomb of the saint, they said, "Receive, O blessed Ninian, that which we offer to thee, a gift hateful indeed, but well fitted to prove thy power. We, of a truth, worn out, fatigued, borne down with sorrow, overcome by weariness, expose it to thy pity. Verily, if it be a gift, favour is due to those who offer it; if it be a burden, thou art fitter to bear it, who hast more power to lighten it. Here therefore let him die or live, let him be cured or let him perish." Having continued to say these and such things with tears, they left the sick child before the sacred relics and went their way. And behold in the silence of the midnight hour, the poor wretch saw a man come to him, shining with celestial light, and glittering in the ornaments of the episcopate, who, touching his head, told him to arise and be whole, and give thanks to God his Saviour. And when he had departed, the wretched being, as if awaking from a deep sleep, by an easy motion twisted each member into its natural place, and having recovered the power of all of them, returned to his home safe and sound. After this he gave himself wholly up to the church and to ecclesiastical discipline, and after being first shorn for the clericate, and then ordained presbyter, he ended his life in the service of his father.

(2. *In a poor man afflicted with scab.*)

On the fame of the miracle being made known, many ran together, each one laying his own trouble before the sacred relics. Among these, a simple man, poor in fortune, but rich in faith and good-will, approached, whose whole body an extraordinary scab had attacked, and so beset all his members that the skin hardening in marvellous fashion closed the courses of the veins, and on every side bound up the arteries, so that nothing but death awaited the patient. The unhappy man, therefore, approaching the body of the saint, offered up most devout prayers to altar, faith, and Lord. His tears flow, sobs burst forth, the breast is beaten, the very bowels tremble. To such faith, to such contrition, neither the merit of the saint nor the pity of Christ were lacking, Who therein glorified His saint and mercifully saved the poor man. Why should I delay longer? The poor Adefridus, for that was his name, did not cease from prayer, until in a few days he was restored to his former health.

(3. *In a blind girl.*)

There was moreover among the people a certain girl, Deisuit by name, who was so tormented with a pain in her eyes that the violence of the disease took away all power of sight, and darkness creeping around her, even the light of the sun was hidden from her. It was painful to the patient and grievous to her sympathizing relations. The skill of the physicians turned to despair; Ninian, the only hope that remained, is applied to. She was led by the hand before that most sacred spot. She is left weeping and wailing; she asketh earnestly; she seeketh anxiously; she knocketh importunately. The compassionate Jesus is faithful to His Gospel promise—" Ask, and ye shall receive; seek, and ye shall find; knock, and the door shall be opened unto you." Therefore to that girl before mentioned the grace which she sought appeared; the door of pity at which she knocked was opened; the health which she sought was vouchsafed; for the darkness was taken away and light was restored. All pain disappeared, and she who had come, led by another to the sacred tomb, returned home guided by her own sight, with great joy of her parents.

(4. *In two lepers.*)

Moreover there were seen to come into the city two men that were lepers, who deeming it presumptuous to touch with the contact of leprosy the holy thing, from some distance implored the help of the saint. But coming to the fountain and holding that to be holy whatever Ninian had touched, they thought to be washed in that laver. O new miracle of the prophet Eliseus! O new cleansing, not of one, but of two Naamans! Naaman came in the spirit of presumption, they in that of humility. He came in doubt, they in faith. The king of Syria doubted, the king of Israel doubted, Naaman doubted. The king of Syria doubted: he doubted and was proud, who sent his leper to be cleansed, not to the prophet but to the king. The king of Israel doubted, who, on hearing the letter read, rent his clothes, and said, Am I God, that I can kill and make alive? Naaman doubted, who, when he heard the advice of the prophet, went away in a rage. Naaman stood in the chariot of pride at the door of Eliseus. These men in faith and humility cry aloud to the mercy of Ninian. Rightly then is that fountain turned into a Jordan, Ninian into a prophet. The lepers are cleansed alike by the touch of the laver, and by the merits of Ninian; and their flesh is restored like the flesh of a little child, and they return to their own healed, to the glory of Ninian, in praise of God, Who worketh thus marvellously in His saints.

But now this is the end of this book, though not the end of the miracles of S. Ninian, which do not cease to shine forth even unto our own times to the laud and glory of our Lord Jesus Christ, who with the Father and the Holy Ghost liveth and reigneth for ever and ever.   Amen.

Here endeth the Life of S. Ninian, Bishop and Confessor.

THE LIFE OF S. KENTIGERN

BY JOCELINUS, A MONK OF FURNESS.

PROLOGUE.

To his most reverend lord and dearest father Jocelinus, an anointed bishop of the Lord Jesus Christ,
Jocelinus, the least of the poor ones of Christ, with the
feeling and reality of filial love and obedience, wisheth
the salvation of body and soul in our Saviour.

Since the fame of thy name, the loftiness of thine
office, the even balance of thy judgment, thy life
which is darkened by no shadow of evil report, thy
long-tried religion, give me sufficient reason for
believing, on diligent consideration, that thou art the
ornament of the House of the Lord, over which thou
dost preside, I have deemed it fitting to offer unto thee
the first-fruits of my gatherings, which are redolent
of the glory and beauty both of thyself and of thy
church. For I have wandered through the streets
and lanes of the city, according to thy command, seeking the recorded life of S. Kentigern whom thy soul
loveth; in whose chair the grace of Divine condescen-

sion, by the adoption of sons, by ecclesiastical election,
by the succession of the ministry, hath caused thy
sanctity to preside. Wherefore I have sought diligently for a life of him, if perchance such might be found,
which with greater authority, with more evident
truth, and with more cultivated style, might be composed, than that which thy· church useth ; because,
as seemeth to most men, it is stained throughout by
an uncultivated diction, discoloured and obscured by
an inelegant style ; and what beyond all these things
any wise man would still more abhor, in the very
commencement of the narrative something contrary to
sound doctrine and to the Catholic faith very evidently
appeareth.   But I have found another little volume,
written in the Scotic dialect, filled from end to end
with solecisms, but containing at greater length the
life and acts of the holy bishop. I confess that I
mourned and took ill that the life of so precious a
bishop, glorious with signs and wonders, most distinguished by virtues and doctrine, should be tainted
by what was perverse or opposed to the faith in its
narrative, or again made exceedingly obscure by barbarous language ; wherefore I determined out of either
book to put together in the way of restoration the
matter collected, and, so far as I might, and by thy
command, season what had been composed in a barbarous way with Roman salt. I deem it absurd that
so precious a treasure should be swathed in vile wrap-
pings, and therefore I have endeavoured to clothe it,

if not in gold tissue and silk, at least in clean linen.
I have endeavoured so to pour the life-giving wine
from the old vessel into the new, that drawing it out
in proportion to the scanty capacity of the vessel may
be desirable to the simple, not useless to those who
are further advanced, and no object of contempt to
those who are richly endowed with sense. The merits
and prayers therefore of the holy bishop aiding me, if
the favour of the Inspirer from on high smile upon me,
I shall so temper the style, that neither shall the work
undertaken by me be obscure by creeping in the dark
from too lowly language, nor, on the other hand, by
aiming on high shall it swell, with pompous words,
beyond what it ought, lest I should seem to have
planted a grove in the temple of the Lord, which He
hath forbidden. Therefore the whole study of this
work, the entire fruit of this my labour, I have deemed
meet to consecrate to thy name, to submit to thine
approbation. If, however, anything be put forth which
is inelegant or insipid, let it be seasoned with the salt
of thy discretion ; if anything sound therein scarcely
consonant with truth, which I do not think there is,
let it be shaped and squared by the rule of thy judgment. If nothing be found failing in either of these
respects, let it be supported by thy testimony and confirmed by thy authority. And in all these things,
if anything proceeding from my pen come to light
otherwise than becometh the subject, be it imputed to
the unskilfulness of my incapacity. If ought shall be
produced worthy of being read, be it ascribed to thine
eminency. But I have nowhere been able to find the

description of the Translation of this saint, nor the miracles performed after his death, which, however, were not noted, perhaps because they escaped the memory of those who were present, or were multiplied beyond enumeration, and which have thus been omitted, that the mass of facts collected might not engender fatigue in feeble readers. May thy sanctity ever live and flourish in the Lord.

Here endeth the Prologue.

HERE BEGINNETH THE LIFE OF S. KENTIGERN,
BISHOP AND CONFESSOR.

CHAPTER I.

THE beginning of the record of the glorious life of the most famous Kentigern, very dear to God and man, a Nazarite of our Nazarene Jesus Christ, is consecrated by that Divine oracle, where the Lord, anticipating by the blessings of His graciousness the holy prophet Jeremiah, announces that he shall be a chosen vessel sanctified to the office of the ministry, by such praise as this—" Before I formed thee in the belly I knew thee : and before thou camest forth out of the womb I sanctified thee, and I ordained thee a prophet unto the nations."[1] Verily, blessed Kentigern, known to God before he was born into the world, bedewed with the grace of election before he came forth from his mother's womb, was in the beginning made great by miracles before he became great, either in bodily form or by his merits. For the Holy of holies began to make him shine forth in the sunlight of virtue in his very origin when sanctified in the womb, and when yet more fully to be sanctified, while enclosed in his mother's breast, that he might prove that the special gift of the Holy Spirit is not constrained by the chain of original sin. I say, that this man, famous for his race and beauty, distinguished in many ways by signs, prodigies, and portents, did the Redeemer of the nations decree to destine as a prophet, yea, as a doctor and head ruler to many nations. Wherefore this most holy one, although he drew his original germ from a royal stem, yet came forth as a rose from the thorn, as an aromatic tree from the filthy ground, for his mother was the daughter of a certain king, most Pagan in his creed, who ruled in the northern parts of Britannia. But when into the land of that region the sound of the announcement of the Christian faith went forth, and the words of saintly preachers advanced into those northern regions from which all evil used to proceed, she heard with her ears those things that were to be heard how the Brightness of the Eternal Light, the Sun of Righteousness, rising by the star of virginity, illuminated the world with the rays of His knowledge and love, and declared salvation to those who were near and to those that were afar off, leading His own into the entire fulness of the truth, more efficaciously, by the argument of evident signs ; straightway her heart was hot within her, and in her meditation that fire was kindled which the Lord sent on earth, and earnestly willed that it should be kindled, and her soul thirsting to come to the recognition of the truth, conceived the engrafted word which could save her soul from eternal death. Though she was not yet washed in the stream of the saving laver, she was running in the way of God's commandments, with an active and open heart. She was occupying herself continually in frequent almsgivings, in devout prayers, in learning and exercising herself in the discipline of the faith of the church, so far as she might for fear of her Pagan father. Yet with a special devotion among these things, she admired the fruitful purity of the Virgin Mother, in admiring it she venerated it, in venerating and loving it she sought to imitate it, and with a certain presumptuous boldness of female audacity willed to be like her in conception and birth, for which she sedulously laboured to entreat the Lord.

After the lapse of some time she was found with child, and her soul did magnify the Lord, simply believing, as she did, that her desire had been accomplished. Now that which was born in her was from the embrace of man, but, as she often, binding herself by an oath, asserted, by whom, or when or in what manner, she conceived, she had no consciousness. But although she was ignorant of the fact of the secret, or it had escaped her memory, by no means should the truth of the affair perish in the mind of a discreet person, nor should scruple arise therefrom ; for, that for the present we may bury in silence what are found in poetic songs, or what we find inserted in histories which are not canonical, when we turn to the sacred volumes, we read in the Book of Genesis that the daughters of Lot not merely furtively secured for themselves the embraces of their father, but actually both by him, when he was inebriated and entirely ignorant of what he was doing, conceived. It is certain moreover that many having drunk the potion of oblivion, which physicists call Letargion, have slept, and have never felt when they suffered incision and sometimes burning of the limbs and the abrasion even of the vitals, and after awaking from the sleep have been ignorant of what was done to them. We have known also that by the sleight of hand of sooth-sayers, maiden chastity has been stormed, and the deflowered one has never known who ruined her. It may be that something of this kind happened to the girl, by the secret judgment of God, that she might not feel the mixture of the sexes, and so, when impregnated, might think herself undefiled.

We by no means think that it was purposeless that this should have been mentioned, since the stupid and foolish people, who live in the diocese of S. Kentigern, go so far as to assert that he was conceived and born of a virgin. But why should we delay at these things? Surely it is both absurd and irrelevant longer to investigate who was the sower or how the seed was ploughed in or sowed, when, the Lord giving the increase, the earth brought forth good and rich fruit—the fruit, I say, of this land, which hath received blessing from the Lord, whereby many generations are blessed by Him, and receive from Him the fruit of eternal salvation.

Meanwhile the woman went about, and her swelling womb began to exhibit to all beholders the sign of her conception. And now the pallor of her countenance, and the swelling of the veins of her throat, and the milk bursting from her breasts, announced that her delivery was at hand. And when this had been instilled into the ears of the king her father, and he had proved the truth of the matter in a more certain examination by sight and touch, he began most earnestly to try to learn from her, now urging her by her fears, now coaxing her by blandishments, who had brought her to the condition in which she was. But she with an oath declared, in the name of Christ, that she was innocent of all intercourse with man. On hearing this the king was moved with greater rage, both because of the name of Christ which sounded in his ears, and because he could not find out the violator of his daughter. Whereupon he swore, and was steadily purposed to keep his righteous judgment, and determined not to swerve from the law handed down from his ancestors in such cases, for the love or the life of his daughter.

CHAPTER II.

Of the Law that was established in those days among the Cambrian people about Girls who committed Fornication.

THERE was a law among that barbarous people, promulgated from a remote antiquity, that a girl committing fornication in her father's house, and found with child, was to be cast down from the summit of a high mountain, and he who sinned with her was beheaded. So among the ancient Saxons, up nearly to modern times, the law remained in force, that every virgin of her own will deflowered in her father's house should be without any remission buried alive, and her lover hanged over her sepulchre. What shall we say to these things, or what can we conjecture concerning them? If such a zeal for chastity burns in the heathen, who are ignorant of the Divine law, solely for decency's sake and the observance of the traditions of their fathers, what shall the Christian do, who is bound to the preservation of chastity by that Divine law? for if the joy of heaven be promised as the reward of the observance, so, on the other hand, for the infraction of that law eternal punishment is now prepared. Behold in these days, both sexes, and every condition, are plunged in every slough of carnal sin, almost with a ready will, and without restraint, because they do it with impunity. And not only is the vile commonalty polluted by this contagion, but even those who are maintained by ecclesiastical benefices, and who betake themselves to the Divine offices, are so much the more impure as they deem themselves more happy. For now the hammerer of the whole earth, even the spirit of Fornication, hath passed over them. They who exhibit in outward form the appearance of sanctity, but deny the power thereof, by their works paying allegiance to the present world, are known by their impure lives to lie to God by their sacred habit and tonsure. Verily they must fear what God threatens by His prophet, saying, "He who hath done iniquity in the land of the saints shall not look upon the glory of the Lord." For now, what is to be bewailed with every flood of tears, that sin of sins, than which nothing more detestable can be conceived, on account of which the sulphurous flame in the five cities, a heavenly judgment, destroyed the guilty, is committed with impunity. Nor can there easily be found one who can chide the perpetrator. For if any one, however rarely, may be discovered, whom the zeal of the Lord's house consumeth, who burneth with the love of righteousness and decency, so that he should seem to censure such monstrous crimes, straightway he is resisted to the face as a sycophant, and condemned by all as guilty of detraction. His mouth is stopped as of one speaking wickedly, his tongue is decreed to be tied up.

Wherefore is this? Plainly, because the body of leviathan, as it is written, is shut up with scales. "One is so near to another, that no air can come between them;" because the criminous and guilty ones, who are the children of the devil, are mutually protected by others who are implicated in the same vice, that the arrow of correction cannot penetrate them. Verily, as I think, this takes place as a proof of their irretrievable damnation, that such men, being given over to a reprobate mind, neither receive, nor will accept, the rod of correction. And the multitude, stained with the same vice, improves them not by punishment, seeing that the many, as well as they themselves, individually burn as if cast into a furnace.

But what shall we say of those on whom the duty is enjoined of binding and loosing, of opening and shutting, who are placed upon a candlestick, that in the House of God they may shine by word and example? Do not the greater part now-a-days exhibit rather smoke than flame, rather stench than brightness? Are they not dumb dogs, that cannot, yea, that will not, bark? When they see manners worse than beastly, they dare not check them, especially since they themselves are confirmed in these habits, nay, in truth, are more wicked. For as with the people so with the priest; as is the subject so is the prelate; nay, they who are first in dignity are first in iniquity; and they who excel in office are deepest in vice. What the Scriptures mystically saith of such is to be feared for them: "And if so much as a beast touched the mountain, it was to be stoned." The beast toucheth the mountain when any one of beastly life mounteth the chair of prelacy, and applieth an impure hand to purifying sacrifices. Yet such is the one who is ordered to be stoned, for that he should be subjected to a severe and grave condemnation is evidently taught to us in the opinions of the holy Fathers. That I should have said this by way of digression will, I pray, be burdensome to no one. The zeal of this Pagan man, who spared not his own daughter, but who for the fault of simple fornication handed her over to so terrible a punishment, should cause great shame to the worshippers of Christ, in planting and propagating modesty.

CHAPTER III.

In what way the Divine mercy saved the Mother of S. Kentigern from the Precipice and from Shipwreck.

ACCORDINGLY the girl aforesaid, by the king's command, was led to the top of a very high hill, called Dunpelder, that, cast down from thence, she might be broken limb by limb, or dashed to pieces. But she, groaning heavily, and looking up to heaven, said in complaining words, "Justly do I suffer this, for that I have done very foolishly, in wishing to be equalled to the most holy, most serene source of salvation, the parent who brought forth her Father. But I beseech thee," she said, "O Mary, blessed among women, pardon the iniquity of thine handmaid, for I have done very foolishly. O mother of mercy, show the light of thy loving-kindness towards me, and free me from the plague which surroundeth me. I beseech thee, O Lady, that as He, the flower of the angelic mountains, without injury to thy snow-white purity, vouchsafed to become in thee the lowly and fertile valley of all virtues, the lily of our valleys, and out of thee, the most firm mountain of the faith deigned to become the stone hewn without hands, which became a great mountain, and filled the whole earth; so deliver me thine handmaiden, though not yet washed in the sacred font, yet firmly believing in thy Son, and resting under the shadow of thy wings, from the imminent precipice, that the blessed name of thy Son may be for ever magnified in the sight of these people. Moreover, I promise the fruit which I bear in my womb to thy Son and to thee, as a special property, to be thy servant all the days of his life."

When she had prayed in this manner, with devout heart and mouth, the servants of the king hurled her from the top of the mountain, as with frequent urgency she invoked Christ and His mother. A wonderful thing occurred, unheard of from ancient times. When she fell she was not bruised, because the Lord supported her with His hand, and therefore she sustained no injury; since, as it seemed to her, like a bird bearing feathers, she came down with easy descent to the ground lest she should dash her foot against a stone. Thanksgiving and the voice of praise sound forth from the mouths of many who beheld these wonderful works of God. The holy and terrible name of Christ is magnified. The innocent one is judged, and not only is to be deemed free from all further punishment, but in every way to be held in veneration. But, on the other hand, the idolaters and adversaries of the Christian faith imputed this not to Divine virtue but to magical arts, and with unanimous voice proclaimed her a witch and a sorceress. Therefore there was a division among the people concerning her. Some said, She is a good woman, and innocent. Others said, Nay, but by her conjuring she deceiveth the people, changeth their countenance, and deludeth their senses.

The crowd therefore in a whirl of words confused itself, but the sacrilegious multitude prevailing, urged the king, who was entirely devoted to idolatry, to dictate a new sentence on his daughter. At length, by the common verdict of the society of the ungodly, and of the adversaries of the name of Christ, it was decreed that that poor little pregnant woman, placed alone in a boat, should be exposed to the sea. In order therefore that the sentence thus determined should be carried into effect, the king's servants, embarking, took her far out to sea, and committing her to fortune alone in a very little boat of hides, made after the fashion of the Scotti, without any oar, rowed back to the shore. They related to the king and to the people, who were waiting the issue of the event, what they had done. But they mocking said, "She calleth herself the handmaid of Christ, and professeth to have the protection of His power, let us see whether her words are true. She trusteth in Christ, let Him deliver her, if He be able, from the hand of death and from the peril of the sea."

But the girl, destitute of all human help, committed herself unto Him alone that created the sea and the dry land, devoutly praying Him, who had before now saved her from the precipice, to protect her from the shipwreck which threatened her. Wonderful to relate, though nothing is impossible with the Lord, that little vessel, in which the pregnant girl was detained, ploughed the watery breakers and eddies of the waves towards the opposite shore more quickly than if propelled by a wind that filled the sail, or by the effort of many oarsmen. For He who preserved unhurt amid the ocean-currents Jonah the prophet, borne within the vast belly of the whale, who by His right hand held up blessed Peter when he was walking upon the waves that he should not be drowned, and who saved from the depths of the sea his co-apostle Paul, who thrice suffered shipwreck, brought the girl safe to the haven of refuge, for the sake of the child which she bore in her womb, whom He predestined to be an excellent captain of His ship; that is, a doctor and good ruler of His Church.

CHAPTER IV.

Of the Birth of S. Kentigern, and his Education, by S. Servanus.

THE girl aforesaid landed on the sand at a place called Culenros. In which place at that time S. Servanus dwelling, taught sacred literature to many boys, who were to be trained to the Divine service. When she had landed on the shore the pains of approaching childbirth seized her. Raising her eyes, she saw at a distance, although in the darkness, the signs of the ashes of a fire near the shore, which perhaps some shepherds or fishermen had left there. She crawled to the place, and as best she might kindled for herself a fire. But when the dawn, the herald of the Divine light, began to brighten, the time was accomplished that she should bring forth. And she brought forth a son, the preacher and herald of the true Light.

Now, at the same hour, while S. Servanus, intent upon prayer after mass in the morning, was drawing in his breath in the delight of Divine contemplation, he heard the companies of the angels chanting their mellifluous praises on high, joying along with whose lauds, he with his disciples, exulting in spirit, strove to sacrifice to the Lord the victims of jubilation by singing, *We praise Thee, O Lord*. On the clerics being astonished at the novelty of the affair, and demanding what had happened, he told them all in order the whole matter, and the hymnings of the angels, sedulously exhorting them to offer the calves of their lips to the Lord. But there were in the neighbourhood shepherds keeping watch over the flocks. And they going forth in the early day-spring, beheld a fire lighted close at hand, and coming with haste found the young woman with her childbirth completed, and the child wrapped in rags, and lying in the open air. They, moved by pity, took care of them by increasing the fire and supplying food, and procuring other necessaries; and bringing them in as suitable way as they could, and presenting them to S. Servanus, related the matter from the beginning.

On hearing this, and seeing the little boy, the mouth of the blessed old man was filled with spiritual laughter, and his heart with joy. Wherefore in the language of his country he exclaimed, "Mochohe, Mochohe," which in Latin means "Care mi, Care mi," adding, "Blessed art thou that hast come in the name of the Lord." He therefore took them to himself, and nourished and educated them as if they were his own pledges. After certain days had passed he dipped them in the laver of regeneration and restoration, and anointed them with the sacred chrism, calling the mother Taneu, and the child Kyentyern, which by interpretation is, The Capital Lord. That this new name, which the mouth of S. Servanus bestowed on him, was not received in vain, shall be clearly set forth in what followeth. Wherefore the man of God educated the child of God, like another Samuel committed unto him and assigned by God. But the child grew, and was comforted, and the grace of God was in him. But when the age of intelligence, and the acceptable time for learning arrived, he handed him over to be trained in letters, and spent much labour and care that he might profit in these things. Nor was he disappointed in his desire in this respect, seeing that the boy, in learning and retaining, well and richly responded to his training, "like a tree planted by the water side, which bringeth forth its fruit in due season." The boy advanced, under the unction of good hope and holy disposition, in the discipline of learning as well as in the exercise of the sacred virtues. For there were bestowed upon him by the Father of Lights, from whom descendeth every good and perfect gift, a docile heart, a genius sharp at understanding, a memory tenacious in recollecting, and a tongue persuasive in bringing forward what he willed; a high, sweet, harmonious, and indefatigable voice for singing the Divine praises. All these gifts of grace were gilded by a worthy life, and therefore beyond all his companions he was precious and amiable in the eyes of the holy old man. Wherefore he was accustomed to call him in the language of his country, "Munghu," which in Latin means "Karissimus Amicus," and by this name even until the present time the common people are frequently used to call him, and to invoke him in their necessities.

CHAPTER V.

Of the little bird that was killed, and then restored to life by Kentigern.

THE fellow-pupils of S. Kentigern, seeing that he was loved beyond the rest by their master and spiritual father, hated him, and were unable either in public or private to say anything peaceable to him. Hence in many ways they intrigued against, abused, envied, and backbit him. But the Lord's boy ever had the eye of his heart fixed upon the Lord; and mourning more for them than for himself, cared little for all the unjust machinations of men. Now a little bird, which, on account of the colour of his body, is called the redbreast, by the will of the Heavenly Father, without whose permission not even a sparrow falleth to the ground, was accustomed to receive its daily food from the hand of the servant of God, Servanus, and by such a custom being established it showed itself tame and domesticated unto him. Sometimes even it perched upon his head, or face, or shoulder, or bosom; sometimes it was with him when he read or prayed, and by the flapping of its wings, or by the sound of its inarticulate voice, or by some little gesture, it showed the love it had for him. So that sometimes the face of the man of God, shadowed forth in the motion of the bird, was clothed in joy, as he wondered at the great power of God in the little creature, to Whom the dumb speak, and the irrational things are known to have reason. And because that bird often approached and departed at the command and will of the man of God, it excited incredulity and hardness of heart in his disciples, and convicted them of disobedience. And this will not seem strange to any one, seeing that the Lord by the voice of a mute animal under the yoke reproved the madness of the prophet, and Solomon, the wisest of men, sent the sluggard to the ant, that by considering her labour and industry, he might cast away his torpor and sloth. Moreover, a certain saint and sage invited his religious to consider the work of bees, that in their little bodies they might learn the beautiful discipline of service. And perhaps it will seem wonderful to some that a man so holy and perfect should take delight in the play and gesture of a little bird. But such should know that perfect men ought sometimes to have their rigours mitigated by something of this kind, that they who mentally approach to God should some-

times descend to our level; just as the bow ought occasionally
to be unbent, lest it be found, from too long tension, nerveless
and useless, at the needful time, in the discharge of the arrow.
Even birds, in passing through the air, sometimes are able to
rise with extended wings, and sometimes, closing them, to
descend towards earth.

Therefore on a certain day, when the saint entered his oratory
to offer up to God the frankincense of prayer, the boys, avail-
ing themselves of the absence of the master, began to indulge
in play with the aforesaid little bird, and while they handled
it among them, and sought to snatch it from each other, it got
destroyed in their hands, and its head was torn from the body.
On this play became sorrow, and they already in imagination
saw the blows of the rods, which are wont to be the greatest
torment of boys. Having taken counsel among themselves,
they laid the blame on the boy Kentigern, who had kept himself entirely apart from the affair, and they showed him the
dead bird, and threw it away from themselves before the old
man arrived. But he took very ill the death of the bird, and
threatened an extremely severe vengeance on its destroyer.
The boys therefore rejoiced, thinking that they had escaped,
and had turned on Kentigern the punishment due to them, and
diminished the grace of friendship which Servanus had hitherto
entertained for him.

When Kentigern, the most pure child, learnt this, taking
the bird in his hands, and putting the head upon the body, he
signed it with the sign of the cross, and lifting up holy hands
in prayer to the Lord, he said, "Lord Jesus Christ, in Whose
hands is the breath of every rational and irrational creature,
give back to this bird the breath of life, that Thy blessed name
may be glorified for ever." These words spake the saint in
prayer, and straightway the bird revived, and not only with
untrammelled flight rose in the air in safety, but also in its
usual way it flew forth with joy to meet the holy old man as
he returned from the church. On seeing this prodigy the heart
of the old man rejoiced in the Lord, and his soul did magnify
the Lord's boy in the Lord, and the Lord, Who alone doeth
marvellous things, and was working in the boy. By this
remarkable sign, therefore, did the Lord mark out, nay, in a
way, presignify, as his own, Kentigern, and announced him
beforehand, whom in after times, in manifold ways, He made
still more distinguished by wonders.

CHAPTER VI.

Of the Fire extinguished through envy by the Companions of
S. Kentigern, and by his Breath brought down from Heaven
upon a little branch of hazel.

IT was the rule of S. Servanus, that each of the boys whom
he trained and instructed should, during the lapse of a week,
carefully attend to arrange the lamps in the church, while the
Divine office was being celebrated there by day and by night;
and for this purpose, when the others had gone to sleep, should
attend to the fire, lest any neglect from default of light should
happen to the Divine service. It happened that S. Kentigern,
in the order of his course, was appointed to this service, and,
while he was doing it diligently and in order, his rivals, (inflamed with the torches of envy, nay, blinded, as it is the pecu-
liarity of perverse men to envy the advance of their betters, to
persecute, to pervert, and to diminish the good which in themselves they have not, nor will to have, nor can have,) on a certain solemn night secretly extinguished all the fire within the
habitations of the monastery and the places in its neighbourhood. Then, as if ignorant and innocent, they sought their
beds, and when about cockcrow, as was his custom, at the
sacred vigils, S. Kentigern arose, as custom required that he
should attend to the lights, he sought for fire everywhere
round about and did not find it.

At length, having found out the wickedness of his rivals, he
determined in his mind to give place to envy, and began to
leave the monastery. But when he had come to the hedge
which surrounded that habitation, returning to himself, he
stood still, and armed his soul to endure perils from false
brethren, and to bear the persecution of the froward. Then
going back to the house, he laid hold of and drew out a bough
of a growing hazel which had come up beside the hedge, and,
enkindled by faith, he besought the Father of Lights to lighten
his darkness by the pouring in of new light, and in a new way
to prepare for himself a lantern by which he might clothe with
healthful confusion those his enemies who persecuted him.
Lifting therefore a pure hand, he signed the bough with the
sign of the cross, and blessing it in the name of the holy and
undivided Trinity breathed upon it. A wonderful and remarkable thing followed! Straightway fire coming forth from
heaven, seizing the bough, as if the boy had exhaled flame for
breath, sent forth fire, vomiting rays, and banished all the sur-

rounding darkness, and so in His light seeing light, he walked into the House of God. God therefore sent forth His light, and led him and brought him unto the monastery, even unto His holy hill and unto His dwelling. And so he went unto the altar of God, who gave joy to his youth by so clear a sign, and kindled the lamps of the church, that the Divine office might be celebrated and finished in due season. Therefore was the Lord his light and his salvation, that he might no longer fear any of his rivals, because He gave sentence for him, and defended his cause against those unjust, envious, and deceitful youths, so that their malice might no more prevail against him.

All were astonished, beholding this great vision, when that torch burnt without injury to itself, as when in olden time the bush which appeared to Moses seemed to be burnt, and yet was not consumed. For it was one and the same Lord who wrought the self-same wonder in the bush and in the twig of hazel; for the Same who destined Moses as a lawgiver for the people of the Hebrews, that he might lead them out of the bondage of Egypt, deigned to destine Kentigern as a preacher of the Christian law, to many nations, that he might rescue them from the power of the devil. In the end that torch was extinguished from heaven, when the lamps of the church had been lighted, and every one more and more wondered, beholding these great things of God. For that hazel from which the little branch was taken, received a blessing from S. Kentigern, and afterwards began to grow into a wood. If from that grove of hazel, as the country folks say, even the greenest branch is taken, even at the present day, it catches fire like the driest material at the touch of fire, which in a manner laps it up, and, influenced by a little breath by the merit of the saint, sheds abroad from itself a fiery haze. And verily it was right that a miracle of this nature should continue, yea, perpetuate itself in his case, who, although in the verdure of the spring-time of life, the delight of the flesh was vigorous, yet inwardly was strong, and all the glory of the world, like the grass of the field, entirely withered because the Spirit of the Lord blew upon it, and the Word of God for ever abiding, by His enlightening consecrated to Himself that hallowed soul and undefiled body, and the fire of the Holy Spirit burnt him up as a whole burnt-offering, accepted as an odour of a sweet savour.

CHAPTER VII.

Of the Cook raised from the Dead by the Prayers of S. Kentigern.

S. SERVANUS had a certain man deputed to the office of the kitchen, who was very necessary for him and for those who dwelt with him, in that he was well qualified and active in that duty, and carefully attended to this frequent ministry. It happened that, seized with a sharp illness, he lay upon his bed, and the disease increasing and running its course, he yielded up the vital spirit. Sorrow filled the heart of the aged man for his death, and all the crowd of his disciples, and all his family, lamented for him, because it was not easy to find another like him for such a service. Fulfilling a natural duty, they consigned his native dust in the womb of the mother of all, and sustained no small loss on account of his decease. On the day after the burial, all the disciples and servants, both those friendly and those jealous, came to S. Servanus, earnestly beseeching him that he should by his prayer summon his Munhu, and compel him by his virtue of obedience, so far as to endeavour to raise his cook from the dead. For the envious ones asserted that the Egyptian magicians, by their enchantments, had shown forth signs from heaven, and, on the testimony of John in the Apocalypse, that the disciples of Antichrist would send down fire from heaven, and that many wizards had in the eyes of all done what seemed wondrous by their occult arts, but that none of the human race could bring back to the breath of life one who was really dead, unless he was a man perfect in holiness.

They persisted, in season and out of season, urging him by persuasive words, to test his sanctity by such a work as this; and that his merit would be proclaimed for ever if he recalled to life one dead and buried. The holy old man at first hesitating to presume to enjoin so unusual a work on the young man, at length, overcome and constrained by their wicked importunity, reasoned with the Lord's young man on the matter with bland words and entreaties, but found him reluctant, asserting that he had not the merit for this. Then S. Servanus adjured him by the holy and terrible name of God, that at least he should try what he could do in such a matter, and this he commanded in the force of holy obedience. The young man then fearing that adjuration, and thinking that obedience was better and more pleasing to God than all sacrifices, went to the tomb where the cook had been buried the day before, and caused the

earth wherewith he was covered to be dug up and cast out.
Falling down therefore alone on the ground, with his face
plentifully bedewed with tears, he said, " O Lord Jesu Christ,
Who art the life and the resurrection of Thine own who faithfully believe in Thee, Who killest and makest alive, Who
bringest down to the grave and bringest up, to Whom life and
death are servants, Who raised Lazarus when he had been four
days dead, raise again this dead man, that Thy holy name may
be blessed and glorified above all things for ever."

An exceedingly astonishing thing followed! While S. Kentigern poured forth copious prayers, the dead man lying in the
dust straightway rose again from the tomb, and came forth,
though bound in grave-clothes, from the sepulchral home.   He
verily arose from the dead as the other arose from prayer, and
along with him, and a large company following him, he proceeded safe and active first of all to the church, to return
thanks to God, then, by the command of Kentigern, he betook
himself to his accustomed duty of cooking, all wondering at
the miracle and praising the Lord.   He, in truth, who was raised
from the dead declared in after times what he had seen of the
punishment of the wicked and the joys of the righteous; and
he converted many from evil to good, while he strengthened in
their holy purpose many who were endeavouring to advance
from good to better.   On being urged by many, he likewise
unfolded the manner of his resuscitation.   He asserted that he
had been reft from things human with unspeakable pain, carried
before the tribunal of the terrible Judge, and that there he
had seen very many on receiving their sentence plunged into
hell, others destined to purgatorial places, some elevated to
celestial joys above the heavens.   And when, trembling, he was
awaiting his own sentence, he heard that he was the man for
whom Kentigern, beloved of the Lord, was praying, and he was
ordered by a being streaming with light that he should be
restored to the body, and brought back to his former life and
health ; and he was sedulously warned by him who conducted
him, that for the future he should lead a stricter life; and in
truth, the self-same cook, assuming holy religion in act and
habit, and profiting and advancing from strength to strength,
lived seven years longer, and then yielding to fate, he was
buried in a noble sarcophagus ; and there was also engraven on
the lid of the tomb how he had been raised from the dead by
S. Kentigern, that by all who saw it or were to see it in time to
come, the Lord, wonderful in His saint, might be magnified.

CHAPTER VIII.

How S. Kentigern departed secretly from S. Servanus, and what sort of a Miracle was wrought at his departing.

WHEN the sanctity of S. Kentigern shone forth, illustrated by such remarkable signs, and the sweet savour of his virtues shed forth far and wide an odour of life, his rivals drew in an odour of death from these life-giving scents, and that very holy opinion of him, which afforded matter of edification to many, was in their case an incentive towards sowing the seed of greater hatred against the saint of God. The boy, prudent in the Lord, knew that the measure of their malice against himself was filled up, and that the inveterate envy that had entered into their bowels and marrow could not be appeased in their unquiet hearts. Nor did he deem it safe to continue longer beside the crowd of venomous serpents, lest perchance he might suffer the loss of inward sweetness. He also weighed the air of popular favour, serenely breathing upon him, and from every side crying "Well done! Well done!" He forthwith proposed to himself to leave the place, that he might in humility forsake the company of those who hated and envied him, and also prudently avoid vainglory. Upon this, after applying himself to the most earnest prayer, he betook himself to the Angel of good counsel, entreating Him that His good Spirit might lead him in the right way, that he might not chance to run or have run in vain. The Lord therefore inclined His ear to the prayers of His servant, revealing to him by the Spirit that the holy intention which had rested in his mind would be well-pleasing in the eyes of the Lord.

He therefore retreated secretly from the place, having the Lord of truth as his guide and protector, in every place. Journeying, he arrived at the Frisicum Litus, where the river, by name Mallena, overpassing its banks when the tide flows in, took away all hope of crossing. But the kind and mighty Lord, who divided the Red Sea into heaps, and led the people of Israel through the same dryshod, under the guidance of Moses, and again turned back to its source the perpetual flowing of Jordan, that the children of Israel might enter with dry footsteps the land of promise under Joshua; and who, at the prayer of Elias, and Eliseus his disciple, divided the same river of Jordan that they might pass dryshod; He Himself now

with the same mighty hand and stretched-out arm divided the
river Mallena, that Kentigern, beloved of God and of man,
might cross on dry ground. Then the tide flowing back in a
very wonderful way, and, if I may so say, being as it were
afraid, the waters both of the sea and of the river stood as walls
on his right hand and on his left. After that, crossing a little
arm of the sea, near a bridge which by the inhabitants is called
the Pons Servani, on looking back to the bank he saw that
the waters which had stood as in a heap before, now flowed
back and filled the channel of the Mallena; yea, were overflowing the bridge aforesaid and denying a passage to any one.[1]

And behold S. Servanus, supporting his aged limbs with a
staff, having followed in pursuit of the fugitive, stood above
the bank, and beckoning with his hand, he cried out lamenting,
" Alas, my dearest son! light of mine eyes! staff of mine old
age! wherefore dost thou desert me? wherefore dost thou leave
me? Call to mind the days that are past, and remember the
years that are gone by; how I took thee up when thou camest
forth from thy mother's womb, nourished thee, taught thee,
trained thee even unto this hour. Do not despise me, nor
neglect my grey hairs, but return, that in no long time thou
mayest close mine eyes." Kentigern, moved with these words
of the aged man, melting into tears replied, " Thou seest, my
father, that what is done is according to the Divine will. We
neither ought nor can we alter the counsel of the Most High,
or fail to obey His will. Besides there is this sea, which
between us as a great gulf is fixed, so that they who would
pass from hence to you cannot, neither can they pass to us that
would come from thence.[2] I pray thee, therefore, have me
excused." Then said the old man, "I pray thee, that by thy
intercession, as thou hast just done, thou wouldest make solid
again the liquid, divide the ground and make it bare, so that at
least I, crossing, might reach thee dryshod. With willing mind
will I become son instead of father to thee, disciple instead of
teacher, pupil instead of guide, so that to the evening of my
days I may be thine own companion." Then again Kentigern,
weeping copiously, replied, " Return, I pray thee, my father, to
thine own people,[3] that in thy holy presence they may be
trained in sacred doctrine, guided by thine example, and restrained by thy discipline. The Rewarder of all reward thee,
for all the benefits which thou hast done unto me, and since
thou hast fought the good fight, even now hast finished thy
course, and hast maintained the faith, living and fruitful, hence-

forth there is laid up for thee a crown of righteousness, which
the Lord, the righteous Judge, will render to thee in the next
world.   But I, destined to the work of the ministry, will go
forth to that which He sent me, who separated me from my
mother's womb, and called me by His grace."

Having said this, and having mutually blessed each other,
they were divided the one from the other, and never looked in
each other's face again in this world.   For Servanus, returning
home, awaited in a good old age the day of his call, and thus
growing old in good days, and being gathered to the holy
fathers, he rested in the Lord, and, like a good labourer in the
vineyard, at even-tide, received the penny of eternal reward from
his Lord.   And what sort of a man, and how great he was, and
in what virtues he shone, a little book written of his Life will
exhibit more clearly to those who read it.   Now the place by
which S. Kentigern crossed became after that entirely impass-
able.   For that bridge, always after that covered by the waves
of the sea, afforded to no one any longer means of transit.
Even the Mallena altered the force of its current from the proper place, and from that day to this turned back the channel
into the river Ledon.   So that forthwith, the rivers which till
then had been separate from each other now became mingled
and united.

CHAPTER IX.

*Of the Sick Man who desired, and sought in prayer, and obtained
from the Lord, that before his death he should see S. Kentigern; and tasted death in his presence, and obtained
sepulture by his forethought.*

THERE was a man of venerable life, Fregus by name, tormented
by much and long sickness.   He lived in a town called Ker-
nach, detained upon the bed of pain, sound in holy conversation, strong in faith, intent upon heaven.   This man, just and
full of holy fear, when the south wind was blowing over his
garden, so that the odours of its breeze might reach him, felt in
his breast a sweetness which proceeded forth from the opinion
he had of the sanctity of S. Kentigern.   Whence also as there
burnt in him the desire, and both heart and eye thirsted, one
would have thought the wish of the holy old man Symeon was
renewed, which he had to see the Lord.   For Symeon, with

panting heart, desired with the eye of the flesh to behold the
salvation of God, Christ the Lord, and Fregus, with firm faith,
unmeasured desires, and frequent prayers, besought of the Lord
that he might see Kentigern, the servant of the Lord Christ.
Christ heard the desire of both, and the ear of God, hearing the
desire of their hearts, fulfilled it.   The desire and joy of
Symeon was fulfilled on the day that Christ was presented in
the Temple for his salvation.   Fregus, for his consolation, saw
and rejoiced in seeing Kentigern on the day that he parted
from S. Servanus.   For Fregus had received a promise from
the Holy Ghost that he should not see death till he had seen
Kentigern, the Nazarite of the Lord.

And when Kentigern had come to the habitation of the holy
sick man, and knocked at the door, the sick man from within,
warned by a Divine oracle, exclaimed, saying, " Open ye the
gates, for the Lord is with us.   The herald of my salvation, promised me by God, and long expected by me, to-day is manifested."
And when he had seen him he rejoiced in spirit, and having
given thanks, he blessed the Lord, and said, " Lord, now lettest
Thou Thy servant depart in peace, according to Thy word, for
mine eyes have seen Thy consolation, which Thou hast prepared
before the face of many people, a light to reveal the true Light
that lighteth every man that cometh into this world, and to
declare the glory of eternal life to the people of these and
many nations."   And turning to him he said again, " Dispose of
my house and my life to-day, and to-morrow attend to my
burial, as it pleaseth Thy providence, the Lord inspiring thee."
Then, by the advice of holy Kentigern, he dispersed abroad
and gave to the poor all the worldly substance he possessed,
and, after making a pure confession, he was anointed with the
oil of remission, and purified with the sacrament of the life-giving
Body and Blood of the Lord, and then he commended his spirit
into the hands of the Lord, and with eyes and hands lifted up
to heaven, he expired during the words of prayer.   Next day
S. Kentigern yoked two untamed bulls to a new wain, in which
he placed the body, whence the spirit had departed, and having
prayed in the name of the Lord, he enjoined upon the brute
beasts to carry the burden placed upon them to the place which
the Lord had provided for it.   And in truth, the bulls, in no ways
being restive, or in anything disobeying the voice of Kentigern,
without any tripping or fall, came by a straight road, along
where there was no path, as far as Cathures, which is now
called Glasgu, along with Kentigern and many others accom-
panying ; and then, with all gentleness, with the burden of the
sacred earth laid on them, a beauteous sight, they halted near

a certain cemetery, which had been long before consecrated by S. Ninian.

Verily, with no less miracle, in no diverse way, with no unequal power, was this chariot, by ruling and threatening, directed to the appointed place by Him who in old time brought from Ekron to Bethshemesh, when Dagon was cast down and broken, the ark of the covenant, which had been taken by the Philistines, placed on a new waggon, and drawn by milch-cows that had never borne the yoke. Therefore the saint in the same place took the holy body down from the wain, and after celebrating his obsequies buried him in that cemetery in which none other man had yet lain. This was the first burial in that place, where afterwards very many bodies were buried in peace. The greatest reverence was paid to the tomb of the man of God; nor did any rash fool dare to trample or pass over it without vengeance, for within the revolution of a year many who trod on it or neglected to pay it honour were smitten down with grievous misfortune, some were even mulcted by death. That tomb is to the present time encircled by a delicious density of overshadowing trees, in witness of the sanctity and the reverence due to him who is buried there.

CHAPTER X.

Of the Two Brothers, one of whom perished by the judgment of God, the other, with all his family, was deemed meet to be blessed by the Lord for many generations.

WHEN the man of God, Fregus, had been buried, S. Kentigern, as was enjoined on him of God by revelation, dwelt in the same place with two brothers, who inhabited the place before his arrival, and framing his life in much sanctity, went on with great virtues unto perfection. One of those with whom he lived was called Telleyr, the other Anguen. But Anguen received God's saint as an angel of the Lord, and loved him with his whole heart, and obeyed his commands with all reverence and veneration, and submitted himself to all his requirements. And not in vain. For the servant of the Lord blessed him in the name of the Lord, and, succoured by that blessing of graciousness, not only he, but all his posterity, received a blessing from the Lord, and mercy from the God of his salvation, seeming to procure it by a sort of hereditary right. For the Lord magnified them in the sight of kings, and

made their name great, like unto the names of those who were
great upon the earth, so that not only by abundance of substance, but by the culture of the Christian religion, they increased and extended themselves in such wise that it was
justly said of them, This is the seed which the Lord hath
blessed, by the merit and prayers of His servant Kentigern.

But the other, by name Telleyr, was very hostile to him,
secretly detracting from his religion, misinterpreting all his
actions, often openly withstanding him, insulting, and injuring
him. Either by minishing from the good he did, or perverting
it, he obscured everything by a sinister interpretation. But
the servant of God had by continual use, accustoming himself,
with blessed Job, to be the brother of dragons and the companion of ostriches, and like Ezekiel to dwell with scorpions,
in patience possessed his soul, and was peaceful with him who
hated peace. But when he spoke of the things that concerned
peace, Telleyr, perverse and ungrateful that he was, only made
himself ready for battle. But God, the Lord of vengeance, the
patient Rewarder, suffered not the injury done to His servant to
go long unrequited. For on a certain day, after many reproaches, by which he had made sad the soul of that righteous
one, he went forth to his work. And because he was very
strong, he placed upon his shoulders a weighty beam, exceeding
the measure of his strength, rejoicing and thinking that he had
acquired the reputation that in bearing burdens he was stronger
than the asses. But when he had gone a little way he tripped
upon a stone and fell, so that, crushed by his burden, he gave
up the ghost, expressing what Solomon says, "Woe unto him
that goeth alone; for he shall have no one to raise him when
he falleth; and again, " He hath fallen once for all, who is
always doing evil."

Kentigern, hearing that his adversary had fallen, lamented
him deeply, and procured for him a place of interment; in this
imitating holy David, the king of the Hebrews, who bewailed
the death of his persecutor Saul, and mourned for him with a
great mourning. But because, according to Solomon, when
the fool perisheth the wise man will be wiser, we have in the
fall of this man a sufficient proof, that we ought not to offend
the servants and friends of God, or dare to inflict on them
molestation, grievances, or injury. For the Elect are the
Temple of the Lord, and the Holy Spirit dwelleth in them.
They are therefore the more to be deferred to, and men should

abstain from injuring them, inasmuch as He who dwelleth in them is most powerful in vindicating their wrongs, and just in rendering justice to those who suffer injuries.

CHAPTER XI.

Of the Election of S. Kentigern, and his Consecration as Bishop.

AND when S. Kentigern, living in the place aforesaid, became fertile in the abundance of many miraculous gifts, it pleased Him who had separated him from his mother's womb, not to leave him under a bushel, but rather to place him on a candle-stick, that, by making his righteousness clear as the light, and his just dealing as the noon-day, he might give light to all that were in the house of the Lord. Therefore, by Divine prompting, the king and clergy of the Cambrian region, with other Christians, albeit they were few in number, came to-gether, and after taking into consideration what was to be done to restore the good estate of the Church, which was well-nigh destroyed, they with one consent approached S. Kenti-gern, and elected him, in spite of his many remonstrances and strong resistance, to be the shepherd and bishop of their souls. He objected to their election of him, that he was not fit on account of his youth; they alleged the gravity of his manners and the affluence of his knowledge and wisdom. He declared that he could not with easy mind endure the diminution of his inward peace and holy contemplation; they alleged, on the other hand, that it was healthful to break in on the sabbath of the life of speculation, for the salvation of many souls. In the end, he judged himself insufficient for the honour which was in truth a burden, but the unanimous voice of all proclaimed that his sufficiency had been proclaimed by God Himself, by many indications of signs and wonders. Invoking therefore a prosperous rule, blessing him in the name of the Holy Trinity, and committing him to the Holy Ghost, the Sanctifier and Distributor of all the orders, offices, and dignities in the Church, they enthroned him; and having called one bishop from Ireland, after the manner of the Britons and Scots of that period, they caused him to be consecrated bishop.

A custom had grown up in Britannia, in the consecration of bishops, only to anoint their heads by pouring on them the sacred chrism, with invocation of the Holy Spirit, and benediction and laying on of hands, which rite these ignorant persons alleged they had received as an institution of the Divine law and an apostolic tradition; whereas the sacred canons ordain that no bishop shall be consecrated without three bishops at least; to wit, one to act as consecrator, who shall say over him who is to be consecrated the sacramental benedictions and prayers for each of the episcopal ornaments, and two others who shall lay on hands along with him, shall be as witnesses, and shall hold the text of the Gospels supported on his neck. Yet although the consecration to which the Britons were accustomed is scantly consonant with the sacred canons, still it is agreed that it does not destroy the power and efficiency of the Divine mystery, or of the episcopal ministration. But because those islanders, as placed beyond the civilized world, on account of the attacks of the Pagans made upon them, were ignorant of the canons, the judgment of the Church, condescending to them, admits excuse for that reason, but in such times as these would never permit such a rite as this to be used by any one without grave censure.

But S. Kentigern, although he was consecrated after this fashion, took pains to correct it in every way possible, as we shall state hereafter. He established his cathedral seat in a town called Glesgu, which is, interpreted, The Dear Family, and is now called Glasgu, where he united to himself a famous and God-beloved family of servants of God, who practised continence, and who lived after the fashion of the primitive church under the apostles, without private property, in holy discipline and Divine service.

Moreover, the diocese of that episcopate was extended according to the limits of the Cambrian kingdom, which kingdom reached from sea to sea, like the rampart once built by the Emperor Severus. This rampart afterwards, by the assistance and counsel of the Roman Legion, in order to keep off the incursions of the Picts, gave way to a wall built in the same place, eight feet in breadth and twelve feet in height; it reaches as far as the Flumen Fordense, and by division separates Scotia from Anglia. Now this Cambrian region, over which S. Kentigern presided as bishop, had once on a time, with all Britannia, accepted the Christian faith in the time of Pope Eleutherius, when Lucius was king; but in consequence of the Pagans from time to time infesting the island, and asserting dominion therein, the islanders, lapsing into apostasy, had cast away the faith which they had received. Many were not yet baptized. Many were stained by the contagion of manifold heresy. Many, in name only Christians, were plunged in the slough of vice of all sorts ; the greatest part of them had been taught by the ministry of men who were unskilled and ignorant of the law of God. Thus all the Provincials required the counsel of a good pastor, and the healing of a good governor. Therefore God, the disposer and dispenser of all good things, provided, promoted, and proposed S. Kentigern as the remedy for all their diseases, the support of their lives, and their example.

CHAPTER XII.

How S. Kentigern conducted himself in the Episcopate ; how he lived and how he taught ; and how he deported himself both openly and in private.

BLESSED Kentigern having taken possession of his government, as he excelled others in dignity, so he sought to exceed them in sanctity. And as he was higher in rank, so he studied to appear more excellent than others in the ordinance of holy virtues and manners. For he deemed it unworthy for himself to crawl upon the ground, or to lie in the depths, who was bound by a Divine command to go up upon the mountain to bring good tidings to Zion. And verily it is unbecoming in him to live in an abject manner, who from his office must announce high things ; wherefore the saint of God, after accepting the episcopal dignity, sought to exercise greater humility and austerity than heretofore in his food, his dress, in watchings, in his hard couches, and in the mortification of his body. And that I may in brief describe his whole life, from the time of his ordination, which took place in the twenty-fifth year of his age, until the extreme term of his life, which lasted the space of one hundred and sixty years,—when he broke his fast after three days, or oftener after four days, he revived rather than recruited his body by tasting the cheapest and lightest foods, such as bread and milk, and cheese and butter and condiments ; and even that, lest the animal frame should entirely fail by the way of this mortality ; yea, rather, to speak more to the purpose, that by mortifying his members which are upon the earth, by the crucifixion of a continual cross, he might by slaying offer himself a living sacrifice, holy, well-pleasing unto God. He abstained entirely from flesh and from blood, and from wine, and from all that could inebriate, like one, nay, like a chief, among the

Nazarites. If, however, at any time it happened that he was on a journey, or dining with the king, he tempered the accustomed rigour of his abstinence. Afterwards, when he returned home, punishing in himself that which he regarded as a gross crime, he increased his abstinence.

CHAPTER XIII.

Of the Mode of Dress of S. Kentigern.

HE used the roughest hair-cloth next the skin, then a garment of leather made of the skin of the goats, then a cowl like a fisherman's bound on him, above which, clothed in a white alb, he always wore a stole over his shoulders. He bore a pastoral staff, not rounded and gilded and gemmed, as may be seen now-a-days, but of simple wood, and merely bent. He had in his hand the Manual-book, always ready to exercise his ministry, whenever necessity or reason demanded. And so by the whiteness of his dress he expressed the purity of his inner life, and avoided vainglory.

CHAPTER XIV.

Of the Couch of S. Kentigern, and his Vigils, and his Bath in Cold Water.

WHAT shall I say of his bed? I hesitate whether to call it a bed or a tomb. He lay in stone hollowed like a monument, having for his head a stone in place of a pillow, like another Jacob. Verily he was a staunch combatant against the flesh, the world, and the devil. Throwing in a few ashes, and taking off his sackcloth, he shook off his drowsiness rather by tasting than taking sleep. And to express myself more clearly, in a certain similitude of a snatch of sleep, he buried himself along with Christ. When he had taken a moderate portion of sleep, he arose in the night, at the beginning of his vigils, and poured forth his soul like water in the sight of the Lord his God. And so with psalms, and hymns, and spiritual songs, celebrating the Lord's night-watches, he exulted in God his Saviour, and was joyful in Him until the second cock-crowing; then, entering upon a fiercer conflict with that great and malignant dragon that, according to the prophet, lieth in the midst of his rivers, he used to strip himself of his clothes, and naked, following a naked Christ, making himself naked and bare, he plunged into the rapid and cold water. Then, verily, as the hart desireth the water brooks, so his soul desired and thirsted for God, the living water; and there, in cold and nakedness, with his eyes and hands lifted up to heaven, he chanted on end the whole Psalter. Thereby made like one of the flock that are ever shorn, which came out from the washing unto Mount Gilead, emerging from the water like a dove bathed in milk, nay, rather as a Nazarite, whiter than snow, brighter than milk, ruddier than ancient ivory, fairer than sapphire, he sat himself to dry his limbs, on the brow of a hill called Gulath, by the water side, near his own home. So having dried his body, and resumed his clothes, as if preparing his going forth in the dawn, he exhibited himself as an ensample to his followers. And this custom of bathing, neither the fire of the glittering lightning, nor hail, nor snow, nor the spirit of storms, ever interrupted, unless a journey necessarily undertaken, or the severest sickness, prevented it; yet even then did he redeem the work by some other divine and spiritual exercise. Wherefore by the continued use of this saving laver, as of a new Jordan, his flesh was restored like the flesh of a little child; because the law of sin, which warreth in the less honourable members, was so weakened, and the fire of concupiscence so mortified and extinguished, that no corruption of the rebellious flesh, either waking or even sleeping, ever polluted or defiled the lily of his snow-white modesty. Nor even did he ever feel its simple motions rage or move within him, for by the grace of Christ co-operating with him, his flesh, with its passions stilled, continued in an almost childlike pure innocence, and verily that holy one grew up before the Lord like an unfading lily, so that once on a time he simply declared to his disciples, that the sight or touch of a most beautiful girl had no more effect upon him than the hardest flint.

CHAPTER XV.

Of the way of Speaking which the Man of God used.

In speaking, however, he was able to control his spirit, and he learned to set a watch before his mouth and to keep the door of his lips, that he might guide his words with discretion. Nor did any one of his words fall lightly to the ground, nor was the word he spoke given to the winds, nor did it return to him in vain. Wherefore he spoke in weight, number, and measure, as the necessary occasion demanded, for his speech was flavoured with salt, suited to every age and sex, for honey and milk were under his tongue, and his cellars were filled with spiritual wine, whence the babe in Christ drank milk from his lips, the more advanced honey, and the perfect man wine, each to his soul's health. In judging and condemning, or in chiding, he had not by him divers measures, nor did he respect the person of man, but he studied the cause, and with the greatest discretion measured forth the degree of ecclesiastical discipline, according to the name of the fault, in due time and place. Yet the saint preached more by his silence than many doctors and rulers do by loud speaking, for his appearance, countenance, gait, and the gesture of his whole body, openly taught discipline, and by certain signs, bursting forth like water, indicated openly the purity of the inner man which lurked there. It is unnecessary to commit to writing his munificence, which spent itself wholly on alms-deeds and works of mercy, for all the substance which the Divine largess had bestowed upon him was the common treasury of the poor.

CHAPTER XVI.

With what a grace he was deemed meet to be adorned, while he was celebrating the Sacred Mysteries of the Mass.

BUT although in the preceding and in similar holy exercises he showed himself as man, and sometimes as above man, it was in celebrating the holy mysteries of the Mass that, in a manner putting off the man and withdrawing himself from earthly things, he put on something like a Divine character, wholly above the human. For while with his hands lifted in the form of a cross he said, "Sursum Corda," he lifted his own unto the Lord as he exhorted others; so from that golden censer of his most pure heart, filled with coals, burning with virtue, and kindled with delight in God, like the brightest and sweetest-savoured incense, his prayer rising to the clouds, penetrating the heavens, and plunging into the light unto which no man can approach, was set forth in the presence of God; so that the Most High Himself vouchsafed by evident signs to manifest to the eyes of mortals that He had accepted it as an oblation, an odour of a sweet savour, well-pleasing to Himself: for very often, as he handled the Divine Sacraments, a snow-white dove, having as it were a golden beak, was seen to light upon his head, and with the transparent fluttering of his wings, like a ray of the sun, to overshadow him and What was laid upon the altar. Frequently also, when he stood sacrificing at holy altars, a luminous cloud overshadowed his head, and occasionally at the time when the Son was being immolated to the Father, he seemed not to stand there, but a fiery pillar by whose brightness the sight of onlookers was blinded. But it was not given to all to know and to behold this ministry, but those only to whom it was granted by the Father of Lights.

Once upon a time, while the Lord's priest was celebrating the mysteries, a sweet-smelling cloud filled the whole house, where many were hearing the sacred mysteries of the Lord, for the odour, exceeding all perfumes, overwhelmed all who were there with exceeding delight, and gave full health to many who were afflicted with various diseases. Verily while I record these things, sorrow filleth my heart, as I see the priesthood defiled in so many ways to-day. While in the meantime I am silent about those who simoniacally come to sacrifice, or with Judas sell the Lord's Body, since forsooth some offer it for a price, I speak of those who, bound by crimes and dissolved in vices, and polluted in body and soul, dare to touch and to contaminate with their impure hands the Sacrifice of Purification. Alas, in how many priests to-day is the stench of foulness rather than the odour of spiritual sweetness observed! O how many more doth the dark whirlwind lay hold of and blind, than doth the shining cloud overshadow! Woe, woe, say I to many to-day for whom the sulphurous flame rather than the surrounding column of fire awaiteth! But now I return unto myself, and to others like unto me, who in any way are discharging the office of their priesthood, and for whom, instead of a snow-white dove at the time of the sacrifice, flies sufficiently tormenting come up out of the river of Egypt—that is the unclean, vain, useless thoughts which rush into the memory, from the imagination of this perishing world. Therefore fearfulness and trembling come upon me, for by the witness of Solomon dead flies cause the ointment to give forth an evil scent, since minds occupied with thoughts of this kind have little experience of what nature is the joy of that inward sweetness, which proceedeth from the visitation of the Holy Ghost.

CHAPTER XVII.

*Of the way in which Holy Kentigern withdrew himself during
    the whole of Lent into more secret places in the Desert, and
    returned to his own Church before Maunday-Thursday, and
    sometimes before Palm-Sunday.*

THE man of God maintained this manner of life here described till an extreme old age, almost all the year round, except
during Lent, for in those days he was accustomed beyond his
ordinary way to walk in a certain newness of life.   Emulating
the fervour of certain of the holy fathers, nay, rather following
the footsteps of Elias and John the Baptist, and of the Saviour
Himself, he retired to desert places every Lent, and so by
withdrawing himself in flight from the sight of the sons of
men, and remaining in a solitude of body and soul, he dwelt
with himself.   There, more freely giving himself up to the
contemplation of God, he rested under the shadow of the Face
of the Almighty, safe from the disturbance of man, from the
strife of tongues and worldly converse.   Therefore sitting
solitary, he lifted himself above himself, and often abiding in
the caverns of the earth, and standing in the entering in of his
cave, and praying, after the great and strong wind and the
earthquake, he heard the still small whisper of thin air breathing upon him, and bathing him in and filling him with unspeakable sweetness.   Wherefore he went about the streets of the
heavenly Jerusalem seeking for himself Him whom his soul
loved, and offering for himself, in his heart, a sacrifice of jubilation, he mortified his most holy members which were upon the
earth.   Offering himself a living victim, holy, well-pleasing
unto the Lord, he afflicted his most innocent body by a continual
martyrdom as a sweet savour.   With what and what sort of
food he sustained his life on those days he revealed to none, or
at least to few, and to these by his episcopal authority he forbade that they should ever reveal the mystery to mortal man.

Yet once he spake, and two of his disciples heard a word not
to be recalled, once only, and simply uttered from his lips.
"I knew," said he, "a certain man, who during Lent sustained
life on the roots of herbs only, and sometimes, the Lord giving
him strength, he passed the whole of that time without the
support of earthly food."   Neither of them doubted that he
spake this of himself; but the man of God suppressed his

name, to avoid vainglory, which he everywhere sought to shun. At length, for a long time before Maunday-Thursday, and after that, on the Saturday before Palm-Sunday, he returned to his home and to his people to fulfil his episcopal office, and he was received by them all as an angel of peace and light. Wherefore he was used to pass that week with his disciples, and on Maunday-Thursday, after the composition of the holy chrism and oil, he washed with his own hands the feet of a multitude of poor men first, and then of lepers, bathing them with his tears, wiping them with his hair, comforting them with many kisses, and afterwards he waited upon the people diligently at table. Then sitting for their consolation with the reconciled penitents at a banquet, he consoled himself and them with spiritual and bodily refreshment. Thereafter from that hour till after the celebration of Mass on Easter Day he always remained fasting. Verily, on Good Friday he crucified himself with the Crucified One with incredible torture, and with scourging, nakedness, and frequent genuflection, scarcely ever sitting down, he passed the day and the night, bearing about in his body the marks of the Lord Jesus, with great affliction of body and soul.

But on the Holy Saturday, as if dead to the world, burying in a double tomb, the true Abraham, the Ancient of Days along with himself, and entering the sepulchre in the abundance of inward contemplation, he rested from all the tumult of this stormy world, except that he appeared to celebrate the Office of the day. Then, renewed in the spirit of his mind, he awaited with the sweet spices of holy virtues so diligently prepared, the most sacred day of the Lord's resurrection. In a way rising again with Christ, he feasted on the Flesh of the Immaculate Lamb, in the unleavened bread of sincerity and truth. And on the day which the Lord had made a day of joy in earth and heaven, he rejoiced with all spiritual joy, and feasted with the brethren and a great multitude of poor. This he also was said to do at the other great festivals. If, however, from urgent necessity, it happened—which seldom, however, actually occurred—that he had to dine with seculars, tasting a little of the food placed before him, he filled the guests with spiritual dainties, and repressing the vain conversation which is apt to prevail at feasts, he concealed his own abstinence under the veil of sacred exhortation.

CHAPTER XVIII.

What a Bright Countenance he had, and what he thought and said about Hypocrites.

HOLY Kentigern in the form of his body is said to have been of middle stature, rather inclining to tallness, and it is asserted that he was of robust strength, capable to a considerable extent of enduring great fatigue in the labours both of body and soul. He was beautiful to look upon, and graceful in form. Having a countenance full of grace and reverence, dove-like eyes, cheeks like the turtle-dove, he attracted the hearts of all who beheld him. His outward cheerfulness was the sign and most faithful interpreter of that inward peace, which flooded all things with a certain contentment of holy joy and exultation, which the Lord bestowed upon him

For himself fleeing from hypocrisy in this or that habit and gesture, he carefully taught his followers to avoid it, and showing by example that hypocrites were the most loathsome class of men, he instructed them in such words as these :—

" Beware, dearest ones," said he to his disciples, " of the vice of hypocrisy, which in a way is the renunciation of faith, the abandonment of hope, the emptying of charity, the suppurating ulcer of chastity, the blinding of truth; it is the poison of sobriety, the fetter of righteousness, the little fox of obedience, the short cloak of patience, and, to speak briefly,'it is the moth of religion, the extermination of virtues, the lurking-place of vices, the asylum of all iniquity, the habitation of crimes. That hypocrisy is the source of all evils, the Lord teacheth where he says that the hypocrisy of the Pharisees is leaven. For as the leaven placed in the food maketh it light, inflated, and acid, so hypocrisy maketh the heart where it reigns empty of religion, inflated and elated with the false praises of men, and sharp, bitter, and sour against the truth of conscience, against the holy, the righteous, and those who seek purity and holiness. And verily, dearest ones, if all sin in itself and by itself be single, hypocrisy alone in itself is double, nay, manifold. For the hypocrite, in his natural colours, seeketh to blind Him who seeth all things, and while turning away his eyes from himself he overshadoweth his vices in the sight of men under the image of a false sanctity. And although other impious, sinful, and criminal men are the members of Antichrist, hypocrites are singularly and specially his followers and forerunners, as the single-hearted, the lovers and followers of truth and purity, are the members and disciples of Jesus Christ. For Antichrist himself, as it is written, shall sit in the temple of God, as if he were God, and by lying wonders show himself that he is God. For the very angel of Satan also transformeth himself into an angel of light, and therefore it is not to be wondered at, that his special servant and member should transform himself into a minister of righteousness, seeing that he is himself a very synagogue of Satan. Believe me what I say unto you in the truth, that the anger of God never rageth more fiercely in the Church than when He makes an hypocrite reign therein on account of the sins of the people. Moreover, in the Apocalypse the persecution is described as more destructive in the pale horse than in the preceding ones, because in truth the Church is much more injured by hypocrisy, which is figured by the pale horse, than in the time of open persecution, whereby the faithful and unfaithful, the just and the unjust, are made manifest, and a multitude of the martyrs receive their crown. Yet, evidently hypocrites, by their gestures and by the ways of the outer man, indicate to those who watch closely and judge all things by the light of the Spirit, of what kind they are. For while they walk after the manner of the turtle-dove, contracting the shoulders, hanging down the head, fixing the eyes on the ground, making long faces, breathing through pinched lips, speaking in a feminine voice, by these very signs they manifest the state of the inner man. For by their steps they make themselves like peacocks, nay, like robbers; by the contraction of their shoulders they show that they shrink from bearing the sweet yoke of Christ and His light burden; by the hanging of their heads and the casting down of their eyes, they demonstrate that their hearts cleave nearer to the dust than to heaven, that they think of the earth, love the earth, and sigh for earthly desires; by turning away their faces, they show that they turn their backs rather than their faces to the Lord, and by their feminine mode of speech prove that they live dissolutely and not like men. I would say that they were like none but jugglers, who exhibit fire, water, men, beasts, etc., in an imaginary way, where there is no reality. But although pretenders and cunning hypocrites, drawing down upon themselves the anger of God, may escape the opinion of those who judge according to appearance, they shall in no ways deceive or escape the even-handed justice of Him who searcheth the heart and the reins. These things, most dear ones," said the man of God, " have I said to you, not to announce what shall be a snare to

you, or that you should not exhibit staid demeanour in countenance, gesture, dress, or discipline, but this in every way I
admonish you to seek the Lord in simplicity of heart, and to
associate internal with external purity everywhere, and in
reality to avoid hypocrisy, and do what you have to do with
spiritual joy. Thus in all your works man shall be edified,
and God glorified, for God loveth a cheerful teacher and doer
of good."

CHAPTER XIX.

*How S. Kentigern converted to the Faith of Christ the people over
whom he presided, and who for the most part had apo-
statized ; and how he brought back to a more correct way of
living those who had profaned the faith by unrighteous
works.*

THEREFORE blessed Kentigern, having undertaken the episcopate, set himself diligently to administer the office laid upon
him, and seeing that the northern enemy, that is, the prince of
this world, had placed his seat in these parts and reigned there,
he took up spiritual arms to fight against him. Accordingly, clad
with the shield of faith, the helmet of hope, the breastplate of
righteousness, girded with the sword of the Spirit, which is the
word of God, he attacked the house of that strong man armed,
and spoiled his goods, supported by the aid of the Lord
of Hosts, who is very strong in battle. And to speak
shortly, neither his foot, hand, nor tongue ceased from the
execution of the work which he had undertaken, from the
working of miracles, from preaching of salvation, till all the
ends of that earth remembered themselves, and turned unto
the Lord. They who were not yet regenerated in the life-
giving waters, like thirsty harts ran to the living fountain of
baptism with burning desire, and they who had fallen away
from the faith, and wandered aside from a sound belief in the
teaching of some heretical sect, on their repenting and returning from the snares of the devil, by whom they were held
captive, and returning unto the bosom of the Church, were
incorporated into Christ, by means of this herald of safety,
teaching them the way of the Lord in power.

Wherefore that renowned warrior began to overthrow the
shrines of demons, to cast down their images, to build churches,
to dedicate them when built, to divide parishes by certain
limits by the cord of distribution, to ordain clergy, to dissolve
incestuous and unlawful marriages, to change concubinage into

lawful matrimony, to bring in as far as he could ecclesiastical rites, and strove to establish whatsoever was consonant with the faith, the Christian law, and righteousness. Wheresoever he journeyed he did it not on horseback, but even to extreme old age, after the fashion of the apostles, on foot. Having arranged all these things in order, he returned home to his own, and there, after his accustomed way, he led a life in the perfection of the highest virtue, remarkable for virtue and miracles, some of which we now venture to write down, because we doubt not that they will be profitable to very many.

CHAPTER XX.

How holy Kentigern, placed in the Plough, under one yoke, a Stag and a Wolf, and how, sowing Sand, he reaped a harvest of Wheat.

THUS, as we have stated, the man of God joined to himself a great many disciples, whom he trained in the sacred literature of the Divine law, and educated to sanctity of life by his word and example. They all with a godly jealousy imitated his life and doctrine, accustomed to fastings and sacred vigils at certain seasons, intent on psalms and prayers, and meditation on the Divine word, content with sparing diet and dress, occupied every day and hour in manual labour. For, after the fashion of the Primitive Church, under the apostles and their successors, possessing nothing of their own, and living soberly, righteously, godly, and continently, they dwelt, as did S. Kentigern himself, in single cottages, from the time when they had become mature in age and doctrine. Therefore these "singulares clerici" were called in the common language Calledei. Thus the servant of Jesus Christ went forth to his work in the morning, and to his labour till the evening, labouring mainly at agriculture, that he might not eat the bread of idleness, but rather in the sweat of his brow afford an example of labour to his own, and have to give to him who was suffering necessity.

It happened once upon a time that he had no oxen whatever, and from the deficiency of these, there being no ploughing, the land lay fallow. When the man of God saw this, lifting up his eyes, he saw on the edge of a neighbouring wood a herd of deer bounding along here and there through the forest. Straight-

way offering up a prayer, by the mighty power of his word he
called them to him, and in the name of the Lord, whom all
dumb unreasoning beasts and all the cattle of the plain obey,
commanded them to be yoked in the place of the oxen to the
plough, and to turn up the earth. They at once obeyed the
command of the man of God, and like tame oxen used to the
yoke ploughed the land, to the astonishment of many. Re-
leased from their work, they went to their usual pastures, and
at the proper hour, like tame and domestic, nay, like trained
animals, they returned to their accustomed toil. Once upon a
time, as the stags were going and returning like domestic
animals, a hungry wolf rushing upon one of the stags, which
was wearied with its labour, and was cropping some food as it
lay upon the green turf, throttled him, and filled his voracious
stomach with his carcase. When the saint learnt this, extending
his hand towards the wood, he said, " In the name of the Holy
and Undivided Trinity, I command that the wolf, who hath
wrought this injury on me who deserved it not, appear before me
to make satisfaction." Wondrous words! more wondrous deeds !
Straightway at the voice of the man of God, the wolf, leaping
forth from the wood, fell howling at his feet, and with such
signs as he could, declared that he begged pardon, and was
willing to make reparation. Whereupon the man of God, up-
braiding the wolf with threatening countenance and word, said,
" Arise, and I command thee, by the authority of God Almighty,
that thou place thyself in the plough in the place of our
labourer the stag, whom thou hast devoured, and applying thyself to the yoke, plough over all that remaineth of the little
field." Verily the wolf obeyed the word spoken by the saint,
and, yoked with the other stag, ploughed up nine acres, whereupon the saint freely allowed him to depart. In this act, it
seemeth to me, that that prophecy of Isaiah, which he spiritually uttered of the time of our Lord's advent, was in a way liter-
ally fulfilled, where he says, " The wolf also shall dwell with
the lamb, and the leopard shall lie down with the kid ; and the
calf, and the young lion, and the fatling together ; and a little
child shall lead them."' Let the reader consider whether it is
more wonderful to see a wolf lying down with a lamb, or
ploughing with a stag. But Kentigern brought this about, being
a most pure little child, meek and lowly of heart in his own
eyes ; yet wrought he not this sign in his own power, but he
did it by the might of that Little One who was born for us, of
the Son who was given for us. Yet it was just that he should

do this bodily, who so often spiritually won back to the yoke of faith and plough of holy conversation many from wolfish cruelty and bloody slaughter, animal fierceness and a coarse life.

Very many gathered together to behold such a sight as this, and marvelled at the unwonted miracle. Whereupon the saint opened his mouth and taught them, saying, "Men and brethren, wherefore wonder ye, beholding this word? Believe me, that before man became disobedient to his Maker, not only all the animals, but even the elements, obeyed him, but now by his transgression all things are turned against him, and the lion teareth, the wolf devoureth, the serpent woundeth, the water drowneth, the fire burneth, the air tainteth, and the earth often, become like iron, consumeth with famine. And in rivalry of this usual evil, not only is man wont to rage against man by sin, but he actually voluntarily rageth against himself. But seeing that many saints are found perfect before the Lord in true innocency, pure obedience, faith, and love, in holiness and righteousness, they receive from the Lord this power, as an ancient, natural, and primordial right, so that they authoritatively command the beasts, the elements, and sundry kinds of diseases and deaths."

While the holy man said this, and more to the same effect, they who heard his words were not less edified by his teaching than astonished by the miracle which they had just beheld. When the field that had been ploughed came to be sown, the saint sought seed and found it not, having given away all his store of grain to feed the poor. Wherefore he betook himself to his accustomed weapons of prayer, and, nothing doubting in faith, taking sand in place of seed, he scattered it on the ground. This being done, in due season the herb grew, the seed germinated, the blade produced the head, and at the proper time brought forth the best and the richest wheat, at which all who heard and saw were struck with the utmost astonishment, and his fame, great before, was mightily increased. Verily this saint, in the power of that Grain of Wheat, Which falling into the earth and dying, and by rising again hath brought to Himself much fruit, gathered corn from the sand which he had sown. Moreover he so wrought with the ploughshare of the gospel in the bowels of holy Mother Church, as in good ground, that he reclaimed many, yea, an innumerable company, of persons, who hitherto had been unstable in mind, blown about by every wind of vain doctrine, whose folly was heavier than the sand of the sea; and in faith and love, and the performance of good works, caused them, by the co-operation of God, to bring forth the fruit of salvation. And these the Supreme Householder deemed meet to be transferred to the heavenly garners, and to be fit for his table.

CHAPTER XXI.

How holy Kentigern, helped by the Divine aid, and causing the force of the river Clud to serve him, without any detriment transferred the Barns of the King, which were full of wheat, to his own dwelling-place.

A CONSIDERABLE time having elapsed, a certain tyrant, by name Morken, had ascended the throne of the Cambrian kingdom, whom power, honour, and riches had persuaded to exercise himself in great matters, which were too high for him. But his heart, as it was on the one hand elevated by pride, so on the other hand it was blinded and contracted by greed. He scorned and despised the life and doctrine of the man of God, in secret slandering, in public resisting him from time to time, putting down his miraculous power to magical illusion, and esteeming as nothing all that he did. But the man of God, once on a time, when he wanted supplies to feed the brethren of his monastery, betook himself to the king, gently hinting at his poverty, and at that of his people, desiring that out of his abundance, according to the injunction of the apostle, he should come to their aid, and supply their wants. But he, elated and haughty, continually reviled him who made his petition, and only inflicted injuries on him who besought support. Then with blasphemous words he said to him ironically, " Cast thy care upon the Lord, and He will sustain thee ; as thou hast often taught others, that they that fear God shall lack nothing, but they who seek the Lord shall want no manner of thing that is good. Thou, therefore, though thou fearest God, and keepest His commandments, art in want of everything, even of thy necessary food, while to me, who neither seek the kingdom of God nor the righteousness thereof, all prosperous things are added, and plenty of all sorts smileth upon me." Lastly, he pressed upon him, " Thy faith therefore is vain, thy preaching false."

But the holy man, arguing on the other side, proved from the testimony of the Holy Scriptures, and from keen assertions of reason, and by examples, that many just and holy men, in various ways, were afflicted by hunger and want in this life ; and that wicked men were exalted by plenty of wealth, the affluence of delights, and the high places of honour. And when with power and clearness he taught that the poor were the patrons of the rich, by whose benefits they are sustained, and that the rich need the support of the poor, as the vines are supported by the elm, the barbarian was unable to resist his wisdom and the Spirit who spake through him, but in a rage answered, "What more desirest thou? If, trusting in thy God, without human hand, thou canst transfer to thy mansion all the corn that is kept in my barns and heaps, I yield with a glad mind and gift, and for the future will be devoutly obedient to thy requests."

Saying this he retired joyful, as if by such an answer as this he had made game of the saint. But when even was come, the holy man, lifting his hands and his eyes to heaven, with many tears, prayed most devoutly unto the Lord. In the very hour in which from the depth of the saint's heart these tears rose up and flowed forth from his eyes, by the will of Him who hath power in heaven and earth, in the sea and in all deep places, the river Clud, coming down, rose and became swollen in flood; then extending beyond its banks, and surrounding the barns of the king which stood there, it licked them up and drew them back into its own channel, and with great power transported them to dry land at a place called by name Mellingdenor, where the saint was at that time accustomed to dwell. Straightway the river ceased from its fury, and controlled within itself the surging waves, for the Lord had placed bounds and bars that they should not pass nor overstep the limits appointed to them. There the barns were found whole and uninjured, and not a sheaf, nay, not a single blade, appeared to be wetted. Lo, in this, though in a different element, we recognise the sign repeated, which we read of as having taken place in the Chaldean furnace, into which the three children, firm in their religion, were cast in bound. For as there the fire had the power of burning only their bonds, and not their bodies or their clothes, so here this water was able to transport the barns filled with corn, but not to wet them. And when the people saw that in the name of the Lord His servant could perform this wonder, they said, Truly great is the Lord, and worthy to be praised, for thus hath He caused His saint to be magnified.

CHAPTER XXII.

*How the aforesaid King Morken, at the instigation of his mili-
tary follower Cathen, struck S. Kentigern with his foot, and
with what punishment both the one and the other were visited.*

AFTER that by the ferrying across of these fruits of the earth,
the rivers of the flood thereof had made glad the city of God,
in which those enrolled as fellow-citizens of the saints, and of the
household of God, were assembled together, to serve the living
God, that faithful and wise servant, made steward over the
mansion of the Great Householder, distributed the measure of
wheat to each of his fellow-servants according to their necessities, and what was over he dispersed abroad and gave to the
poor, nor did he send empty away any one in want who begged
of him.   But the aforesaid King Morken, though very rich and
great in the eyes of men, yet being the vile slave of Mammon,
bore ill the loss, as it seemed to him, of his stock of corn, and
took scandal to his soul from that Divine sign whence he
ought to have derived joy and gladness for his own advantage.
Just as the solar ray is pleasant and agreeable to healthy eyes,
and lends its aid to their sight, yet ministers the material of
darkness to the unhealthy, and to those under the influence of
hemlock : therefore, his eye being consumed because of fury,
he belched forth many reproaches against the holy bishop,
calling him magician and sorcerer, and he commanded that if
ever again he appeared in his presence he should suffer severely
as one that had made game of him.   The reason for this was
that a very wicked man, who was the king's confidential friend,
Cathen by name, had urged him on to hatred and injury of the
bishop, because the life of the good is usually hateful and
burdensome to the wicked ; and the mind that inclineth to evil
easily listeneth to one who persuadeth it to that which pleaseth it.
For every wicked leader, according to the Scripture, hath all
his servants wicked, and very often chooseth as counsellors the
men who into the ears of those who willingly listen to unjust
things will pour the poisonous whisper, and diligently blow
up with inflated accusations the fire of malice, adding fuel to
make the flame burn the higher, lest it should be extinguished
to their detriment.
   But the man of God, wishing by wisdom to extinguish
malice, approached the presence of the king rather in the spirit

of meekness than with the rod of severity, and instructing and warning him after the manner of a most gentle father, sought to correct the folly of a son; for he knew that by the sweetly sounding tones of the harp of David the madness of Saul had been mitigated, and that, according to the sentence of Solomon, the king's wrath is appeased by patience. But the man of Belial, like the deaf adder that shutteth his ear and listeneth not to the charmer, charm he never so wisely, acquiesced not in the warning words, which were the words of safety. Nay, excited by fiercer madness, he rushed upon him, struck him with his heel, and smote him to the ground upon his back. But the saint of God, being raised by the bystanders, that his doctrine might be known by his patience, bore most patiently both the hurt and the dishonour, committing his cause to the vindication of the Supreme Judge, and then he departed from the presence of this sacrilegious king, rejoicing that he was deemed meet to suffer contumely for the word of the Lord.

The instigator of this sacrilege, Cathen, laughing loudly, mounted his horse, and seemingly triumphing over the saint, departed full of joy. And behold judgment went forth from the face of the Lord, to do justice on behalf of His servant who had been injured. He had not gone far from the crowd that was assembled in that place, when the prancing steed on which he was seated, striking his foot on some sort of stumbling-block, fell down, and his rider, falling backward, broke the neck which he had erected loftily against the servant of the Lord, and expired before the gate of the king his master. But a swelling attacked the feet of the king, pain followed the swelling, and then succeeded death; so expiring in the royal town which from him was termed Thorp-morken, he was buried. But the disease was not destroyed or buried in the succession of that family. From the beginning of that time, for the future, the weakness ceased not, and a gout was handed down hereditarily, and this family takes after the father, not in face or in habit of the body, but in disease. For the fact that the race of that king was destroyed by this sort of disease, by the witness of death, indicateth how God, Who is jealous for His own and the avenger of such, visiteth the sins of the fathers upon the children for many generations, and how great is the retribution which He inflicteth upon the proud.

After this, for many days he enjoyed great peace and quiet, living in his own city of Glasgu, and going through his diocese;

because the Divine vengeance, shown forth upon his persecutors, supplied to others a motive of fear, reverence, love, and obedience towards the saint of God, and gave him the opportunity of doing whatsoever he desired for the service and glory of God.

CHAPTER XXIII.

How holy Kentigern, avoiding the snares of those who laid wait for his death, departed from the confines of his country, and betook himself to Saint David, who was dwelling in Menevia.

WHEN some time had passed, certain sons of Belial, a generation of vipers, of the kin of the aforenamed King Morken, excited by the sting of intense hatred, and infected with the poison of the devil, took counsel together how they might lay hold of Kentigern by craft, and put him to death; but fearing the people, they did not dare to do that evil deed openly, because all held him for a teacher, bishop, and shepherd of their souls, and loved him as an angel of light and peace. In many ways they laid great wait for him, that they might suddenly shoot him with arrows; but the Lord became unto him a tower of strength, that his enemies, the sons of wickedness, should not triumph over him. At last, binding themselves together by a solemn oath, they determined among themselves that in no way would they fail in carrying out the resolve by which they had conspired to compass his death; and that for the fear of no man would they pass over one unjust and treacherous word to which they had agreed against him. And when the man of God had learnt this, although he could meet force by force, he thought it better for the time to quit the place and to give place unto wrath, and to seek elsewhere a richer harvest of souls, rather than to bear about with him a conscience seared as with a hot iron, or even darkened by the death of any man, however wicked. For the blessed Paul, the chosen vessel, gave him the ensample of acting similarly, seeing that when at Damascus he saw a death without fruit impending over him, he sought the basket and the rope to escape and to avoid it, and yet afterwards at Rome willingly submitted to it with great gain.

At last, instructed by Divine revelation, he journeyed from those regions towards Menevia, where at that time the holy Bishop Dewi, like the morning star when it with its rosy countenance heraldeth the day, was shining forth in his episcopal work. Wheresoever the saint went, virtue went forth from him to heal many. And when he had come to Karleolum, he heard that many among the mountains were given to idolatry, or ignorant of the Divine law. Thither he turned aside, and, God helping him, and confirming the word by signs following, converted to the Christian religion many from a strange belief, and others who were erroneous in the faith. O how beautiful on these mountains were the feet of him who brought glad tidings, that published peace, that brought good tidings of good, that published salvation, that said unto Zion, Thy God reigneth. He remained some time in a certain thickly planted place, to confirm and comfort in the faith the men that dwelt there, where he erected a cross as the sign of the faith; whence it took the name, in English, of Crosfeld, that is, Crucis Novale. In which very locality a basilica, recently erected, is dedicated to the name of blessed Kentigern; and to exhibit his sanctity, he is not doubted to have been distinguished by many miracles.

Turning aside from thence, the saint directed his steps by the sea-shore, and through all his journey scattering the seed of the Divine word, gathered in a plentiful and fertile harvest unto the Lord. At length, safe and sound, he reached Saint Dewi, and found in him greater works than had been reported by fame. But the holy Bishop Dewi rejoiced with great joy at the arrival of such and so great a stranger. With eyes overflowing with tears, and mutually embracing, he received Kentigern as an angel of the Lord, dear to God, and retaining him for a certain time in his immediate vicinity, always honoured him to a wonderful extent. Therefore these two sons of light dwelt together, attending upon the Lord of the whole earth, like two lamps burning before the Lord, whose tongues became the keys of heaven, that by them a multitude of men might be deemed meet to enter therein. Those two saints were united together opposite each other, like the two cherubim in the holy of holies in the temple of the Lord, having their faces bent down towards the mercy-seat. They lifted their wings on high in the frequent meditation upon heavenly things; they folded them down in the ordination and arrangement of earthly things. They touched each other mutually with their wings, as by the instruction of each other in the Doctrine of Salvation, and in the alternate energizing of virtues they excited each other to a more earnest advance in sanctity. Thus these saints, either mentally rising up unto God, or being made useful to us, have left to posterity an example of laying hold of and labouring so as to attain to eternal life.

And when Saint Kentigern had abode there some time, the fame concerning him shining forth, ran through the ears and mouths of the many, and led him to much familiarity and friendship, not only with the poor, the middle class, and the nobility of that land, but even with King Cathwallain, who reigned in that country. For the king, knowing him to be a holy and righteous man, heard him willingly, and after hearing him, did much which concerned the good of his own soul. And when, on the occasion of the king from time to time inquiring, he expounded the causes why he left his native land, and said he would wish to live near, and have the means of building a monastery where he might unite together a people acceptable of God, and devoted to good works, the king replied, "My land is in thy sight: wheresoever it suiteth thee, and seemeth good in thy sight, there construct the habitation of thy dwelling-place, there build thy monastery. Yet, as it seemeth to me that it is more suitable for thee than any other, I assign to thee a place, Nautcharvan, because it aboundeth in everything suited to thy purpose." The man of God rendered profuse thanks to the king, and chose for his building and habitation that place which had been before marked out for him by Divine intimation. Then, giving his blessing to the king, he departed: and bidding farewell to S. Dewi, after mutual benediction, he betook himself to the place aforesaid, with a great multitude of disciples who had flocked to him, preferring to lead with him a lowly life in a foreign land to living without him luxuriously in their own.

CHAPTER XXIV.

How S. Kentigern, following a Boar which led the Way,
found a fitting place.

THUS the most holy Kentigern, separated from Saint Dewi as to bodily presence, but by no means withdrawn from his love and from the vision and observation of the inner man, gave no sound sleep to his eyes, nor quiet rest to his eyelids, until he found a place fit for building a tabernacle to the Lord, the God of Jacob. With a great crowd of his disciples along with him, he went round the land and walked throughout it, exploring the situations of the localities, the quality of the air, the richness of the soil, the sufficiency of the meadows, pastures, and woods, and the other things that look to the convenience of a monastery to be erected. And while they went together over abrupt mountains, hollow valleys, caves of the earth, thickset briers, dark woods, and open glades in the forest, as they went along, they discoursed as to what seemed necessary for the occasion, when lo and behold a single wild boar from the wood, entirely white, met them, and approaching the feet of the saint, moving his head, sometimes advancing a little, and then returning and looking backwards, motioned to the saint and to his companions, with such gesture as he could, to follow him. On seeing this they wondered and glorified God, who worketh marvellous things, and things past finding out in His creatures. Then step by step they followed their leader, the boar, which preceded them.

When they came to the place which the Lord had predestinated for them, the boar halted, and frequently striking the ground with his foot, and making the gesture of tearing up the soil of the little hill that was there with his long tusk, shaking his head repeatedly and grunting, he clearly showed to all that that was the place designed and prepared by God. Now the place is situated on the bank of a river which is called Elgu, from which to this day, as it is said, the town takes its name. Then the saint, returning thanks, adored the Almighty Lord on bended knees; and rising from prayer he blessed that place and its surroundings in the name of the Lord. After that, in testimony and sign of salvation, and in earnest of the future religion erecting a cross, he there pitched his tents. The boar, however, seeing what was done, came near, and by his frequent grunts seemed to ask somewhat of the bishop: then the saint, scratching the head of the brute, and stroking his mouth and teeth, said, " God Almighty, in Whose power are all the beasts of the forest, the oxen, the birds of the air, and the fishes of the sea, grant thee for thy conduct such reward as He knoweth is best for thee." Then the boar, as if well remunerated, bowing his head to the priest of the Lord, departed, and betook himself to his well-known groves.

On the following night, as the man of God, intent on heavenly things, lifted up his hands in the sanctuary, and blessed the Lord, it was revealed to him from on high that he was to inhabit

that place, and there construct a monastery, in which the sons
who were scattered abroad might be gathered into one, so that
coming from the east and from the west, from the north and
from the south, they might be deemed meet to sit down with
Abraham, Isaac, and Jacob in the kingdom of heaven, and
that God Himself would be the protector and guardian of the
place, and of them that dwelt therein. And on what truth that
revelation rested the successful event effectually showed; for
in the morning he revealed to others the Divine oracle that
had been shown to him, and cheered on the souls of those who
heard him to set about building. For like bees making honey,
they yielded not to sloth, but all in the sweat of their brows
toiled diligently at the work. Some cleared and levelled the
situation; others began to lay the foundation of the ground
thus levelled; some cutting down trees, others carrying them,
and others fitting them together, commenced, as the father had
measured and marked out for them, to build a church and its
offices of polished wood, after the fashion of the Britons, seeing
that they could not yet build of stone, nor were so wont to do.

While they were hard at work, and the building was increasing on their hands, there came a heathen prince, Melconde
Galganu by name, with his soldiers, and along with them a
great multitude of people. The man, fierce and ignorant of God,
in the indignation of his wrath demanded who they were, and
whence they came, and how they had dared to do all this
upon his land. The saint, humbly replying to the interroga-
tion, answered that they were Christians from the northern
parts of Britannia, that they had come thither to serve the
living and true God. He asserted that he had begun the mansion there by the permission, nay, through the kindness of King
Cathwalain, his master, in whose possession he believed the
place to be. But he, furious and raging, ordered them all to
be expelled from the place, and that whatever had been built
should be pulled down and scattered; and so he began to
return to his own home. Therefore the man departed, breathing threatenings against the servants of Christ, and behold the
hand of the Lord in chastisement touched him, and he was
smitten with a sudden blindness. And yet, as was clear in
the end, this did not happen to no good purpose, for on him
that sat in outer darkness the true morning star shone,
and the external light being for a time taken from him, drew
him forth from the darkness and shadow of death into the light
of truth. Wherefore inwardly enlightened and induced by

penitence, he caused himself to be carried by his people to the man of God, and began most devoutly to entreat, that by his prayers he would dispel the darkness, and wash him in the font of salvation.

Verily the saint, who endeavoured not to be overcome by evil, but to overcome evil by good, willed to return to the man good for evil; so after beginning with prayer, he laid his healing hand on the blinded man in the name of the Lord, and signing him with the cross of salvation, turned his night into day, and again after the darkness poured into him the hoped-for and eagerly-desired light. Thus the Lord smote that He might heal, and making the new Paul out of the old Saul, He blinded him that He might give him light. No sooner therefore was he restored to sight than he was dipped by the holy bishop in the saving water, and henceforward he became an active and devoted fellow-worker in all that he desired at his hand. Taking an account of all his possessions, he bestowed them on S. Kentigern, with royal munificence, for the construction of his monastery, and, aided by this assistance, he rapidly brought what he had commenced to perfection. He established the Cathedral Chair of his bishopric in the church of that monastery, of which diocese the greater part of the country was that which by his preaching himself had won to the Lord. In truth he led back to the way of salvation a countless number of men who were either ignorant of the Christian faith, or averse from it, or degraded by profane doctrine, or deteriorated by wicked works. And by his labours he turned vessels of wrath into vessels of mercy, vessels of dishonour into vessels of the glory of God. For he went forth from his monastery to exercise his episcopal office, travelling through his diocese as time permitted. But as he never found where the foot of his desire could long find rest, he returned to the much-loved quiet of his monastery, like the dove to the ark, from the face of the deluge of the world; yet he bore with him the olive-branch with its green leaves, for he received the fruit of that peace and mercy which he preached to others.

CHAPTER XXV.

With what number of brethren his Monastery flourished, and how the holy boy Asaph carried fire without injuring himself.

THERE flocked to the monastery of the man, old and young, rich and poor, to take upon themselves the easy yoke

and the light burden of the Lord. Nobles and men of the
middle class brought to the saint their children to be trained
unto the Lord. The tale of those who renounced the world increased day by day both in number and importance, so that the
total number of those who enlisted in God's army amounted
to 965, professing in act and habit the life of monastic rule
according to the institution of the holy man. He divided this
troop that had been collected together, and devoted to the
Divine service, into a threefold division of religious observance.
For he appointed 300, who were unlettered, to the duty of
agriculture, the care of cattle, and the other necessary duties
outside the monastery. He assigned another 300 to duties
within the cloister of the monastery, such as doing the ordinary work and preparing food, and building workshops. The
remaining 365, who were lettered, he appointed to the celebration of Divine service in church by day and by night;
and he seldom allowed any of these to go forth out of the
sanctuary, but ever to abide within, as if in the holy place
of the Lord. But those who were more advanced in wisdom
and holiness, and who were fitted to teach others, he was
accustomed to take along with him, when, at the urgent demand either of necessity or reason, he thought fit to go forth
to perform his episcopal office. But dividing into troops and
choirs those whom he had appointed for the service of God,
he ordained that as soon as one choir had terminated its service in the church, immediately another entering should com-
mence it, and that again being concluded, a third should enter
to celebrate. Thus the sacred choirs being conveniently and
discreetly arranged so as to succeed in turn, while the work
of God was celebrated perpetually, prayer was regularly
made to God without ceasing of the church there; and by
praising God at every time, His praise ever resounded in
their mouths. Very excellent things were said in that and
of that city of God, for as it became the habitation of all who
were joyful therein, so one might well apply the prophecy of
Balaam : "How goodly are thy tents, O Jacob! and thy taber-
nacles, O Israel! As the valleys are they spread forth, as
gardens by the river's side."

There flourished in that glorious monastery holy and perfect
men, like Jacob, strong wrestlers against the world, the flesh,
and the devil; by faith, love, and contemplation incessantly
bent upon the vision of God, like true Israelites, fruitful in
good works, humble in their own eyes, and therefore like the

well-wooded valleys fragrant with sacred thought, and bedewed with the showers of the Scripture, and thus, also, like
the cedars by the waters, glorious in all these many virtues and
wonders.

Among them was one Asaph by name, distinguished by
birth and by looks, shining forth in virtue and miracles from
the flower of his first youth. He sought to follow the life and
teaching of his master, as the reader of a little book of his
Life may learn at greater length, from which I have thought
fit to insert into this work one miracle, because the perfection
of the disciple is the glory of the master. Once upon a time,
in winter, when the frost had contracted and congealed everything, S. Kentigern, according to his custom, had recited the
Psalter in the coldest water, naked, and having resumed his clothes
had gone out in public, he began to be vehemently oppressed
by the power of the cold, and so in a way to become entirely
rigid, so that people might clearly see what was of himself and
what was of the power of the Divine condescension. For in
that, naked in the waters without being frozen, he was able for so
long a time to endure the icy rigour, men might learn how that
in the frail vessel of the human body the Divine virtue worked ;
and that when clothed in skins and other clothes he became
rigid from the cold, human frailty is recognised. Wherefore the holy father ordered the boy Asaph to bring fire to him
whereat he might warm himself. The Lord's little boy ran to
the oven and requested that coals might be given to him.
And when he had not wherewith to carry the burning thorns,
the servant, either in joke or seriously, said to him, " If thou
wishest to take the thorns, hold out thy dress, for I have not
at hand that in which thou mayest carry them." The holy
boy, strong in faith, and trusting in the sanctity of his master,
without hesitation, gathering together and holding up his dress,
received the living coals in his bosom, and carrying them to
the old man, cast them down in his presence out of his bosom,
but no sign of burning or corruption appeared in the dress.
The greatest astonishment therefore seized all those who beheld
it, on seeing that fire carried in a dress had not in the least
burnt combustible fabric. A friendly dispute concerning this
sign took place between the holy father and his disciple, for
the one side seemed to be maintaining his ground by assertions
to which the other could not assent; the bishop ascribed to
the innocence and obedience of the boy, the performance of the
miracle; the boy asserted that it had taken place for the merit

and sanctity of the prelate, obeying whose command, and trusting in whose holiness, he had dared to attempt it. And indeed
without prejudice I think that the miracle is to be attributed
to the merits both of the one and of the other, of each wise one,
inasmuch as each of them had all along from the earliest years
preserved pure the members of his body, which is the clothing
of the soul, in virgin chastity, and that from their heads the
oil of Divine charity never was lacking: rightly, to express the
innocency of either, did the dress of the disciple fail to exhibit
injury or damage. For if the flame of impure love had been
hidden in their bosoms, according to Solomon's opinion their
clothes would have been burnt. And if their garments had
been mingled with blood; that is, if the members of their
bodies had been stained with the pollution of itching lust from
the will of the flesh and the blood, doubtless, according to
Isaiah, it would have been the presage of burning and the food
for fire. But holy Kentigern, who had always held dear and
beloved the venerable boy Asaph, henceforward ever from that
very day regarded him as the dearest and most loved of all,
and raised him as soon as he could to holy orders. At the due
season he delegated to him the care of the monastery, and
made him his successor in the episcopate, as we shall relate
further on.

CHAPTER XXVI.

*How he saw S. David crowned by the Lord in Heaven, and what
he predicted about Britannia.*

ONCE upon a time, as the man of God continued longer and
more intently occupied in prayer than usual, his face became
as it were fire, so as to fill the bystanders with wonder and
ecstasy. They beheld his countenance as the countenance
of an angel standing among them, and as they saw his face
shining like that of another Moses, astonishment and admiration seized them all. When his prayer was over, he
withdrew himself apart and gave himself up to the most
vehement grief. His disciples, understanding that his sorrow
could not be without a great reason, approached him with fear
and trembling, and humbly besought him, if it were permis-
sible, and not displeasing to his paternity, to reveal to them the
cause of such copious tears. The saint was silent for a time,
but on their persevering and knocking at the ears of that most
pious father, he at length gave way, and answered to this effect:
" Be it known unto you, dearest sons, that the most holy

Dewi, the honour of Britain, the father of his country, the most precious carbuncle of prelates, hath just left the prison of the flesh rich in merits, hath been introduced among the splendours of the saints, and hath penetrated into the Holy of Holies. I say unto you, believe me, that not only hath a multitude of angels flooded in light received him with heavenly music into the joy of the Lord his God, but the Lord Jesus Christ Himself, meek and lowly of heart, hath in my sight gone out to meet him at the gates of paradise, and crowned him with glory and honour. Behold like a matchless light to his generation, and a most brilliant star which shone forth in word and in example, he hath become present to every one under his charge that calleth upon him, so as with delight to shine for Him Who made him, and assist all who ask his protection, who apply to him for help, and who celebrate his sacred memory. And truly, dearest ones, it is right for me to rejoice in the glory of such a father, who loved me full well; but that ardent affection of devoted love for him permitteth me not to abstain from tears. For know that the world of Britain, deprived of such a light, of so tender a patron, and of one so powerful before God and the people, will feel the absence of him, who ever placed himself between that region and the sword of the Lord, half drawn on account of the wickedness of those that dwell therein, lest when entirely drawn from its sheath, it should smite them even to utter destruction. The Lord will surely hand over Britannia unto strange nations, who know not God, who in religion are pagans; and the island shall be emptied of its indigenous inhabitants, and the religion of the Christian Law shall be scattered until the appointed time; but again, by the mercy of God the Mediator, who overruleth all things, Christianity shall be restored as in the beginning, yea, in a way better than before." These things spake the saint, and was silent, and fear came upon all who heard him, and a shower of tears bedewed them. But they, wishing over and above to be assured as to the fact, having called a messenger, they sent him to the Church over which S. Dewi presided as bishop, and they found that the saint had left this world in the same hour in which the man of God, instructed by the Divine oracle, had announced it to them. And in this matter, it must be considered how great was the merit of that man in the sight of God, who, either with the eyes of the body or those of the soul, was deemed meet to behold such glory, and to deliver a prophecy concerning the Britons and Angles so true, which all England was able by a faith that was sight to verify.

CHAPTER XXVII.

How S. Kentigern went seven times to Rome, and consulted the
blessed Gregory about his condition.

THE blessed Kentigern, knowing that Britain in many provinces was smitten with many stripes by the Gentiles, and that
the Church of God established therein was by idolaters in
many ways reft and torn from the faith of Christ; discovering
moreover that it was frequently assaulted by heretics, and that
there were therein many things contrary to sound doctrine, and
alien from the integrity of the faith of our holy mother the
Catholic Church, set himself for a long time to deliberate
within himself what cure he ought to apply to all these evils. In
the end, he determined in his mind to visit the seat of Peter
founded on a rock; and to prevent the tares growing up in the
good wheat, he resolved by the wholesome teaching of the Holy
Roman Church, and by acknowledging the oracles of the faith,
to cast out every scruple of doubt from his mind, so as to be
able to arrive by certain guidings at the light of the truth.
For Britain, during the reign of the most holy king Lucius, in
the papacy of Eleutherius, by the preaching of the most excellent
teachers Faganus and Divianus and others, whom Gildas the
wise, the historian of the Britons, commemorateth, received the
faith of Christ. It preserved that Christianity thus received
whole and undefiled till the time of the Emperor Diocletian.
Then the moon was turned into blood, and the flame of persecution against the Christians burnt brightly through the whole
world. Then that scourge, inundating Britain, vehemently
oppressed it, and pagan hands, mowing the first-fruits of the
island, namely, Alban, took him out of the midst to be recorded
in the Book of the Eternal King; and an innumerable company
of others shortly after, voluntarily, and in ignorance, it offered
to heaven.

From that time the worship of idols began to spring up and
increase in that island, bringing in rejection and forgetfulness of
the Divine law. But Christianity after this somehow revived and
flourished; however, time went on, and first the Pelagian heresy
prevailing, and then the Arian creeping in, defiled the face of the
Catholic faith. This, however, sprang up again and flourished
when these heresies were cast down and conquered by Saint Ger-
manus, Bishop of Auxerre, a man truly apostolic, and made

glorious by many miracles. Yet forthwith the invasion of the neighbouring Picts and Scots, hostile to the recognition of the name of Christ, drove away entirely both the faith and the faithful from the northern part of Britannia. Finally, Britannia was conquered by the Angles, still pagans, from whom it was called Anglia. The natives being driven out, it was given over to idols and idolaters. The indigenous inhabitants of the island, however, fled either across the sea into Little Britain, or into Wales, and though banished from their own land, all of them did not entirely abandon their faith. But the Picts, first mainly by S. Ninian, and then latterly by SS. Kentigern and Columba, received the faith. Then lapsing into apostasy a second time, by the preaching of S. Kentigern, not only the Picts, but also the Scots, and innumerable people gathered from the different parts of Britain, were, as we have said already, and shall say more at length hereafter, either turned to the faith or were confirmed therein.

However, holy Augustine, noted for his monastic life and habit, and other servants of God, religious, were sent commissioned to England by the most holy Pope Gregory, who, rich in the showers of sacred preaching, and glittering in the lightning power of miracles, either by themselves or by their disciples converting the whole island to Christ, and fully instructing them in the rules of faith and the institutes of the holy fathers, filled the whole land of Anglia with the sweet savour of Christ.

On account therefore of Britain being crushed by so many misfortunes, Christianity so often obscured, and even cast down, at different times diverse rites were found in her contrary to the form of the holy Roman Church and to the decrees of the holy fathers. In order, therefore, that he might learn and be able to meet and to remedy all these evils, blessed Kentigern, going forth from the monastery of which we have made mention, betook himself seven times to Rome, and brought home what he learnt there, in so far as the correction of Britain required it; but as he was returning for the seventh time he was attacked by a most grievous malady, and got home with the greatest difficulty.

One of his visits was made to Rome during the time that blessed Gregory presided on the apostolic seat, a man truly apostolic in office, authority, life, and doctrine, and the special apostle of England, for the English are the sign of his apostleship. He was as a vessel of solid gold adorned with every manner of precious stone, and was called Golden Mouth, be-

cause in expounding great parts of the Scripture he made it
clear by the most lucid and polished style. His memory is
as the work of the apothecary in making up the unguent, and
as music in a banquet of wine, because by his honeyed writ-
ings, by his hymns composed according to the laws of music,
he gladdened, and by his canonical institutions he strengthened
and adorned, the house of God, the holy Catholic Church,
diffused throughout the world. To this most holy Roman
Pontiff he laid bare and declared in order his whole life, his
election to the episcopate, his consecration, and all the events
that had happened to him. But the saintly Pope, inasmuch
as he was strong in the spirit of counsel and discretion, filled
with the Holy Ghost, and knowing him for a man of God, and
full of the grace of the blessed Spirit, confirmed his election and consecration, because he knew that both had come
from God. And on the bishop on many occasions seeking it,
and with difficulty obtaining it, he supplied what was wanting
to his consecration, and destined him to the work of the
ministry enjoined on him by the Spirit of God. Holy Bishop
Kentigern, having received the apostolic absolution and benediction, returned home, bearing with him the codes of canons,
many other books of Holy Scriptures, as well as privileges, and
many relics of the saints, and ornaments of the Church, and
whatever lends grace to the house of the Lord. And he gladdened
his own by his return, as well as by many presents and religious
gifts.[1] He dwelt there for some time in great peace and (godly)
conversation, and ruled holily and firmly both his see and his
monastery with great care.

CHAPTER XXVIII.

*What by the revelation of the Spirit he knew of two Clerics, and
what happened to them according to his prediction.*

IT happened that the holy bishop felt it his duty, by ordaining clergy, to confer sacred orders, and to promote some to the
priestly office. Among others there was brought to him a
certain cleric, of elegant form, of great eloquence, of much
learning, by birth a Briton, but educated in the Gauls. When
the saint saw him, he summoned the archdeacon, and ordered
him to be straightway removed and separated from the clergy.
For there seemed to the eyes of the saint a sulphurous flame

to proceed from the bosom of that clerk, and an intolerable smell to offend his nostrils. By this vision, through the revelation of the Holy Spirit, he was made aware of the vice which reigned in his body. For he was, as was then made known to the man of God alone, and afterwards to all, habitually guilty of that most disgusting crime for which the Divine vengeance overthrew in fire and sulphur, and utterly destroyed, the sons of unbelief in the Five Cities. Then said the saint to those who stood around him, "If the sacred canons forbid women, on account of the infirmity of their sex, to which in noways is blame attached, to be promoted to the rank of the priesthood, much more is it our duty to banish from a rank and office so sacred, men who pervert their sex, who abuse nature, who in contempt of their Master, in degradation of themselves, in injury of all creatures, cast off that in which they are created and born, and become as women. Nowhere read we of punishment exercising a graver vengeance than against that monstrous race of men among whom that execrable crime first began. Not only did it overthrow those cities, with the inhabitants thereof, with fire, on account of the burning of evil passion, and with sulphur, on account of the stench of that abominable sin, but it also turned them into a place horrid to the sight, full of sulphur and bitumen and horrible smells, receiving nothing living into itself, having indeed on its banks trees that produce fruits externally sound, but inwardly full of smoke and ashes, shadowing forth an image of the torture of hell. And this indeed sufficiently distinctly exhibiteth how so execrable a pleasure is to be held in abhorrence, and how horrible and how much it is to be avoided of all men in this life, and in the future with what torment it will be visited; while the fire expresseth the heat of passion, the sulphur the ill savour of the crime, the bitumen the adhering effect of the vice, the smoke the blindness of heart in this world, and in the world to come the unquenchable flame, the intolerable stench, the indissoluble chains, the horror of darkness and eternal death." After this the cleric aforesaid departed by the way that he came, and, as the report goeth, he died, cut off by a sudden destruction.

When the holy man had finished his office and was returning home, there met him among the rest a cleric, a most eloquent foreigner. The man of God, beholding him, glanced at him with burning eye, and asked who he was, and whence he was, and wherefore he had come into these parts. He asserted that he was a preacher of the truth, teaching the way of God in truth, and that he had come into these parts for the salvation of souls. But when the saint had conversed with him he convicted him of being intoxicated with the poison of the Pelagian pestilence. Willing therefore that he should rather return than perish, he warned and reasoned with him to renounce the pernicious sect, but found his heart stony as to conversion. Then the saint ordered him to be expelled from his diocese, and denounced him as the son of death, and that the death of body and soul was in his gates. He remembered also the saying of the apostle, "A man that is an heretic, after the second admonition, avoid; knowing that he that is such is subverted." The same son of hell, expelled from these borders, departed, and trying to cross a certain river, choked in the waters, he descended into hell, and thus by an evident proof illustrated the exceeding trustworthiness of the veracious prophecy of the most saintly man.

CHAPTER XXIX.

How the Divine vengeance smote the adversaries of S. Kentigern, and how it bore down upon his countrymen who had fallen away from the faith.

HITHERTO we have related as carefully as we could what S. Kentigern did when he withdrew from his own country, and when he dwelt in a foreign land. Let us point by point henceforth turn back and show what his adversaries suffered, how he returned to the Cambrian region, and what he did there.

After that the man of God yielding to malice departed, his enemies were not long permitted to triumph over his absence. For the Lord visited them with heavy hand and hard arm, and with fury poured out, holding over them a rod that watched for evil and not for good, smiting them with the blow of an enemy, and with cruel chastisement, even to destruction. For the night obscured some of them, and a gloom of blindness followed; others were attacked by paralysis, which enfeebled all their strength, and rendered them actually effete so far as concerned their bodily strength; others an incurable madness, proceeding as far as death, seized; others a contagious leprosy devoured or struck down, tainting them, and making them, as they breathed in their half-alive bodies, like unto the dead in a state of putrefaction. Very many of them became epileptic, and exhibited a dreadful spectacle to those who beheld them. Some one way, some another, were consumed by every kind of incurable disease, and gave up the ghost. So great and so sudden was the indignation of the wrath of God, that all those who had known their power and great numbers hissed over them, saying, " Wherefore hath the Lord done thus unto this people ? since, behold, suddenly they have come to an end, and perished on account of the iniquity which they wrought against the holy one of the Lord, striving to take away from the earth his life and memory."

Even his countrymen had quickly abandoned the way of the Lord, which the good shepherd and true teacher had shown unto them, and, like dogs returned to their vomit, had fallen into the rites of idolatry. But not with impunity ; for from them the heavens, the earth, the sea, and all that are therein, withdrew their obedience, use, and wonted aid, so that, according to the Scripture, the very world itself seemed to fight against these foolish ones ; and the elements seemed not able to bear with equanimity the absence of so great a man exiled from that land ; for according to the words of the prophecy, " All men have departed, all the cattle died, the heaven above was as brass, and the earth as iron, devouring the inhabitants thereof ; and a consuming famine prevailed for a long time over all the earth."

But when the time of having mercy had arrived, that the Lord might remove the rod of His fierce anger, and that they should turn unto Him, and He should heal them, He raised up over the Cambrian kingdom a king, Rederech by name, who having been baptized in Ireland in the most Christian manner by the disciples of S. Patrick, sought the Lord with all his heart, and strove to restore Christianity. And truly it is a great sign of the Divine pity, when the Lord constituteth for the government of the holy Church, and for the dominion of the earth, rulers and kings who judge righteously, live holily, seek the good of their people, and execute judgment and justice on the earth. So, moreover, on the other hand, it is an evident proof of the wrath of God when, for the sins of a people, he causeth a hypocrite to reign, when he calleth the king apostate, and the leaders unjust, as it is written in Job, and when, according to the prophet, he giveth kings in His indignation, and princes in His fury.

CHAPTER XXX.

*How holy Rederech, by messengers and letters, invited S. Kenti-
gern to return to his own see in Glasgu ; and how the holy
prelate, taught by the Divine oracle, assented to the king's
petition.*

WHEREFORE King Rederech, seeing that the Christian religion
was almost entirely destroyed in his kingdom, set himself zeal-
ously to restore it.   And after long considering the matter in
his own mind, and taking advice with other Christians who
were in his confidence, he discovered no more healthful plan
by which he could bring it to a successful result, than to send
messengers to S. Kentigern to recall him to his first see.
The fame of the saint going forth smote on the ears and
mind of the king, for his light could not be hid, although it
shone in the more remote regions.   The king, therefore, sent
forth messengers to the holy prelate with letters deprecating
refusal, and warning, praying, exhorting, and adjuring him
by the name of God, as a shepherd, not any longer to with-
draw his care from the sheep of his pasture, long desolate and
destitute, by any further absence, lest he should expose them to
be carried off and torn by the open mouth of the infernal wolf ;
but rather to hasten forth and meet them before they were swallowed by the throat of the roaring lion seeking whom he might devour, since there is none but he who could deliver, or ought more
justly to do so.   He declared that it was wrong that the spouse
should desert his bride, the shepherd his flock, the prelate his
church, for the love of whom he ought to lay down his life, so
as not to become a hireling.   He showed also that they who
had sought his life had perished by the just anger of God, and
he swore that in all things, as a son to his father, he would
obey his will, his teaching, and his commands.
On receiving this, the holy father was silent, nor did he on
that day return any definite answer, for he had prepared to
nourish his grey hairs to the evening of his life, and to end his
days, in that glorious monastery which he had raised with long
and great labour, and to lay him down to sleep, and to take
his quiet rest in the sight of those, his sons, whom he had begotten in the gospel, and brought forth in Christ.   But because
he sought not his own, but the things that are of Jesus Christ,
and came not to do his own will, but the will of Him who sent
him, as it could be done in heaven, respecting himself, in himself, and towards himself, he submitted himself entirely to the

disposition of God. And while on the following night he was engaged in prayer, and was consulting the Lord on this matter, the angel of the Lord stood beside him, and a light shone in the place of the oratory where he then was, and he smote him on the side and commanded him to rise. And on his standing up, the heavenly messenger said unto him, " Go back to Glasgu, to thy church, and there thou shalt be a great nation, and the Lord will make thee to increase among thy people. Thou shalt truly acquire unto the Lord thy God a holy nation, an innumerable people to be won unto the Lord thy God, and thou shalt receive an everlasting crown from Him. There thou shalt end thy days in a good old age, and shall go out of this world unto thy Father which is in heaven. Thy flesh shall rest in hope, buried with glory and honour, much dignified by the frequent visit of the peoples, and by the exhibition of miracles, till in the last day, by receiving from the hand of the Lord a double robe, thou shalt possess a twofold reward at the general resurrection." Having said this, the angel that appeared to him and who addressed him, departed; but he, weeping copiously, gave thanks unto the Lord, frequently saying, " My heart is ready, O God! my heart is ready for whatsoever may please Thee."

CHAPTER XXXI.

How the Saint addressing his disciples about his return, appointed S. Asaph as his successor in the government.

AND when the day dawned, having called his disciples together, he said unto them, " I speak as a man unto you, dearly beloved; I desired, after long thought and deliberation, according to the infirmity of my flesh, that these mine aged eyes should be closed by you, and that my bones should be hidden in the womb of the mother of all, in the sight of all of you. But since the life of man is not in his own power, it is laid upon me by the Lord that I should return unto mine own church of Glasgu; nor ought we, nor dare we, nor will we, contradict the words of the Holy One, as Job saith, nor in any wise go against it; but rather in all things obey His will and command, even to our life's end. Do you, therefore, most beloved ones, stand firm in the faith. Quit you like men and be comforted, and seek always that everything be done in charity." These, and many things like these, he said in their presence, and lifting his hand he blessed them. Then, with the unanimous consent of all, he appointed the afore-mentioned S. Asaph to the government of the monastery, and by the petition of the people, and by canonical election, the successor of his bishopric; and after that he delivered a profound sermon at great length, of faith, hope, and charity, of mercy and justice, of humility and obedience, of holy peace and of mutual forbearance, of avoiding vice and of acquiring virtue, of observing the institutes of the holy Roman Church, of the regular discipline and exercises which he had established, to be observed by them all, and, in fact, of constancy and perseverance to the end in all good things.

When the sermon was over he enthroned S. Asaph in the cathedral see, and again blessing and taking leave of them all, he went forth by the north door of the church, because he was going forth to combat the northern enemy. After he had gone out, that door was closed, and all who witnessed and heard of his egress and departure bewailed his absence with great lamentations. Hence a custom grew up in that church that that door should never be opened, save once a year, on the day of S. Asaph, that is, on the Kalends of May, for two reasons,— first, in deference to the sanctity of him who had gone forth, and next, that thereby was indicated the great grief of those who had bewailed his departure. Therefore, on the day of S. Asaph, that door is opened, because when he succeeded to S. Kentigern in the government, their mourning was turned into joy. Of that monastery, a great part of the brethren, to the number of 665, in no ways being able or willing to live without him so long as he survived, went away with him. Three hundred only abode with S. Asaph. Surrounded by such a troop as this, as if compassed by the host of the court on high, he returned to fight the old enemy, and to drive him out from the region of the earth where the apostate angel had placed his seat. And truly those who accompanied him were counted by such a number, and by multiplying the senary exercise of good works, by fulfilling the decalogue of the law, arrived at the centenary perfection of virtues, and maintained the quinary guard over the discipline of the senses, so far as they could.

When King Rederech and his people had heard that Kentigern had arrived from Wallia into Cambria, from exile into his own country, with great joy and peace both king and people went out to meet him. On account of his arrival there sound in the mouths of all thanksgiving and the voice of praise and joy; while from the lips of the holy bishop there issued "Glory to God in the highest, and on earth peace to men of good-will."

CHAPTER XXXII.

Of the Devils miraculously driven away, and of the place where he stood to preach, and of the fertility of the land which ensued.

BLESSED Kentigern, on seeing the gathering together and approach of a great multitude hastening towards him, rejoiced in spirit, and therefore offering up thanks, he knelt down in prayer. When he had finished it, he arose and, in the Name of the Holy Trinity, blessed the assembled multitude. Then, as if fortifying the bystanders with the sign of the holy cross, he spake as follows :—" I command that all those who envy the salvation of men, and oppose the Word of God, in the power of the same, depart instantly from hence, and oppose no obstacle to them who shall believe." Whereupon, with exceeding speed, an immense multitude of phantoms, horrible in stature and appearance, coming out of that crowd, fled away in the sight of all ; and a great terror fell on those who beheld them. The holy bishop, comforting them and strengthening them, laid bare the natures of those in whom they had believed, and encouraged the hearts of all who stood around to believe in the living God ; for by clear reason he showed that idols were dumb, the vain inventions of men, fitter for the fire rather than for worship. He showed that the elements in which they believed as deities, were creatures and formations adapted by the disposition of their Maker to the use, help, and assistance of men. But Woden, whom they, and especially the Angles, believed to be the chief deity, from whom they derived their origin, and to whom the fourth day of the week is dedicated, he asserted with probability to have been a mortal man, king of the Saxons, by faith a pagan, from whom they and many nations have their descent. His body, he continued, after many years had passed, was turned into dust, and his soul, buried in hell, endureth the eternal fire.

By these and similar arguments casting forth the worship of idols from their hearts, he proved to them the Almighty God, Three and One, to be the Creator of all things from the very beauty of the visible creation ; and after that, preaching to them the faith that is in Jesus Christ and the Sacraments of faith, he shewed by the most true and lucid demonstrations that there is none other name under heaven, believing in which men may be saved, but only the Name of our Lord Jesus Christ. And when he had, by the instruction and dictation of the Spirit, taught much that referred to the Christian faith, in the place which is called Holdelm, ·the ground on which he sat, in the sight of all, grew into a little hill, and remaineth there unto this day. Therefore, they who had come together, beholding so great and sudden a miracle, obeying the word of faith in their inmost soul, firmly and faithfully believed that Jesus Christ is God, Who had revealed himself to them by His servant Kentigern. Eagerly, therefore, men and women, old men and young men, rich and poor, flock to the man of God to be instructed in the rules of faith; after being catechised, they renounced Satan and all his pomps and works, were washed in the saving laver in the Name of the Holy Trinity; and so anointed with the sacred chrism and oil, and incorporated into the body of the Church, they became members of Christ.

Wherefore the bishop rejoiced with great joy, for that a great salvation had been made, and mighty happiness increased among that people; nor was there less joy in the presence of the angels of God in heaven, for that so great a multitude had turned unto the Lord. Appropriately by such a sign as the elevation of the mountain in the commencement of his preaching, did the Lord deem right to magnify His saint, who by that very preaching effectually brought all to believe, as unto the very mountain, compact and fruitful, in which the Lord was well pleased to dwell. That very Stone, first cut without hands from the mountain, grew up into a high mountain and filled the face of the earth,—for the omnipotent God, born of the Virgin, without human passion, was manifestly shown forth in the breadth of this world. Verily, Christ is that Hill exalted on the top of the mountains, even the Lord Himself, that surpasseth all the power and greatness of the saints; in whose ways, paths, and light, by the instruction of Kentigern, these nations walked much more devoutly and consistently than that carnal house of Jacob, who, loving darkness rather than light, and wandering away from the ways of truth, refused to be enlightened by the illumination of the Supreme Light.

After that the inhabitants of Cambria had turned to the Lord and were baptized, all the elements, which in vindication of the Divine justice had seemed leagued for its ruin, put on a new face towards them for the salvation of body and soul. For as the Lord turning away from the apostates, and opposing them by forbidding the dew to fall, commanded his clouds not to rain upon the earth, and summoned a famine which desolated them, so turning to them that had returned to Him, He commanded the heaven to yield its rain, and the earth to give forth the green herb, and to produce its fruit for those who dwelt thereon. Thus by the Lord causing His face to shine upon them, the sun was felt warmer than usual, the vault of heaven clearer, the air more healthy, the earth more fruitful, the sea more calm, the abundance of all things greater, peace more confirmed, the face of all things more joyous, and therefore the devotion of all in the maintenance of Divine worship was more profuse.

CHAPTER XXXIII.

How King Rederech conceded to him power over himself and his posterity.

Now King Rederech, seeing that the hand of God was good to him, and was operating according to his desires, was filled with great joy. And he made no delay in exhibiting openly the inward fervour which animated his soul. For, stripping himself of his royal robes, on bended knees and hands joined, with the consent and advice of his lords, he gave his homage to S. Kentigern, and handed over to him the dominion and princedom over all his kingdom, and willed that he should be king, and himself the ruler of his country under him as his father, as he knew that formerly the great Emperor Constantine had done to S. Silvester. Hence the custom grew up for a long course of years, so long as the Cambrian kingdom lasted in its own proper rank, that the prince was always subject to the bishop. Frequently was the word again and again asserted by the king, that not in vain, but of set purpose had he been called Kentigern by S. Servanus, because by the will of the Lord he ought to become the head lord of all; for "Ken" is "caput" in Latin, and the Albanic "tyern" is interpreted "dominus" in Latin.

S. Kentigern, thus made a new Melchizedech, hesitated not to accept what the king had so devoutly offered for the glory of God, because he foresaw that in the future even this would be for the advantage of the Church. He had also a privilege sent him from the Supreme Pontiff, that he should be subject to no bishop, but rather should be styled and actually be, the vicar and chaplain of the Pope. But the king, in return for the honour and glory he bestowed upon the holy bishop, received grace for grace, and greater honours and wealth from the Lord.

Moreover, his Queen Languoreth, long bowed down by the disgrace of continued barrenness, by the blessing and intercession of the saintly bishop, conceived and brought forth a son, to the consolation and joy of his whole kindred ; and the saint baptizing him, called him Constantine, in remembrance of the act of his father which he had done to him in resemblance of that which the Roman Emperor Constantine had done to S. Silvester, as has been already stated. He grew up a boy of good disposition, in stature and grace, beloved of God and man, and by hereditary right, when his father yielded to fate, succeeded him in the kingdom, but always subject to the bishop like his father before him. And because the Lord was with him, he overcame all the barbarous nations in his vicinity without bloodshed, surpassing all the kings that had reigned before him in Cambria, in riches, glory, and dignity, and, what is better still, in holiness. So that, famed for merit, and finishing his course in peace, he was deemed meet to triumph over the age, and to be crowned with glory and honour in heaven ; so that to the present day he is called S. Constantine by many. We have said this by anticipation, because we have mentioned Constantine as being born by the prayers of S. Kentigern, and baptized and educated by him. The holy bishop Kentigern, building churches in Holdelm, ordaining priests and clerics, placed his see there for a certain reason for a time ; afterwards, warned by Divine revelation, justice demanding it, he transferred it to his own city Glasgu.

CHAPTER XXXIV.

How many nations the Saint, at one time by himself, at another by his Disciples, cleansed from the foulness of Idolatry, and how he was distinguished for many miracles.

THE blessed Kentigern, like a burning torch in those days, was diligent, by the radiant flames of his virtues, and the burning and shining word of God, to illuminate the souls that were blinded by the darkness of ignorance, to kindle in the cold the love of God, and to burn up and so clear away the thorns of sins and the tares of vices, which according to the ancient curse had spread over the earth and covered it. There was none that could easily hide himself from his heat. For he carefully visited his diocese, and taking away all strange gods from the midst of them, cast forth all the ceremonies of foreign worship, and so preparing the way for the Lord, and making the paths of our God straight, he brought the whole of Christianity there into a better state than it had been before.

Then the warrior of God, consumed with the fire of the Holy Spirit, like a fire that burneth the wood, and like the flame setting on fire the mountains, after he had converted what was nearest to himself, that is to say, his diocese, going forth to more distant places, cleansed from the foulness of idolatry and the contagion of heresy the land of the Picts, which is now called Galwiethia, with the adjacent parts; and amid shining miracles, bringing it back to the rule of truth, he amended, as far as lay in his power, whatsoever he found contrary to Christian faith or sound doctrine. In all these things the fervour of his devotion was not turned away, but his hand was stretched out still to greater actions, and to the increase of the honour and glory of the Most High, his feet having been shod with the preparation of the gospel of peace.

For he went to Albania, and there with great and almost unbearable toil, often exposed to death by the snares of the barbarians, but ever standing undeterred, strong in the faith (the Lord working with him, and giving power to the voice of his preaching), he reclaimed that land from the worship of idols and from profane rites that were almost equal to idolatry, to the landmarks of faith, and the customs of the Church, and the laws of the canons. For there he erected many churches, and dedicated them when erected, ordaining priests and clerics; and he consecrated many of his disciples bishops. He also founded many monasteries in these parts, and placed over them as fathers the disciples whom he had instructed.

In all these matters, his spirit, always panting for the salvation of the many, never rested till, as a glorious standard-bearer of the Lord's host, and as a wrestler of unconquered mind, he fought the battles of the Lord. Therefore he sent forth those of his own, whom he knew to be strong in faith, fervent in love, known for doctrine, lofty in religion, towards the Orchades, Noruuagia, and Ysalanda, to announce to the dwellers therein the Name of the Lord and the Faith of Christ, for that in those places the harvest indeed was great, but there were no labourers; and seeing that he was now old and unable to go himself, he willed that this work should be accomplished by his disciples.

All this being duly done, he returned to his own church of Glasgu, where, as elsewhere, yea, where, as everywhere, he was known to shine in many and great miracles. For wheresoever his lips disseminated the knowledge of salvation, the virtue of God, working in His servant, exhibited the manifold power of marvels. For he restored sight to the blind, hearing to the deaf, the power of walking to the lame, speech to the dumb, reason to the insane. He drove away fevers; he cast out devils from the bodies of those possessed by them; he gave strength to the paralytic; healing to the lunatics; cleansing to the lepers, and cure to all sorts of sicknesses. But in such works as these was his daily wont, his accustomed play, his assiduous custom, which in a way became common from so constant occurrence, and which have not been written down, lest the quantity of them brought together should engender weariness. In many other ways also were many sick men taken to the bishop to be healed by the touch of the hem of his garment, frequently by mouthfuls of food and drink given and received; and sometimes men borne in a bed were healed by the shadow of his body as he passed along, like another Peter.

CHAPTER XXXV.

How the Lord kept his Clothes untouched by any drops of rain, or snow, or hail.

ALTHOUGH the hand of the Lord worked by blessed Kentigern many miracles not commonly vouchsafed to other saints, He wrought one work in him in particular at which all men did wonder. For as all bear witness who knew the man, as well as those that conversed with him, that never in his life were his clothes wetted with drops of rain, or with snow or hail pouring upon him and falling to the ground. For often, standing in the open air, while the inclemency of the weather increased, and the pouring rain flowed in different directions like bilge-water, and the spirit of the storm raged around him, he from time to time stood still, or went whither he would, and yet he always continued uninjured and untouched by a drop of rain from any quarter. And not on him alone did the Lord vouchsafe to exhibit this prodigy, which was the Lord's doing, and wonderful in the eyes of all, but the whole company of his disciples going along with him, by his merits, oftentimes, though not as in his own case always, experienced the same grace in themselves and for themselves. For the sanctity of the holy doctor Kentigern, who was bedewed with Divine grace, was to his followers for a shadow in the day-time from the heat, and a refuge, and for a covert from the storm and tempest.

So let no one disbelieve that the Lord bestowed the blessing of the miracle which we have described on His most devout servant, to the praise of His own most holy Name, and to commend his sanctity, since, in a manner like to this—nay, in a manner greater than this—He vouchsafed in the desert a boon to the whole Hebrew people to show that they had found favour in His eyes. For, as we read, the garments of that people were not worn or destroyed by time; the garments of this man alone were never wetted with the drops of rain from heaven. Therefore to none let this seem incredible; for, as the Lord says, all things are possible to him that believeth, and with the Lord there is nothing impossible. In like manner, the sign which in the smiting of Egypt, as we find written in a certain place concerning the children of Israel, we know to have been frequently repeated in the case of blessed Kentigern. For when darkness overwhelmed the whole land of Egypt, and thick darkness the people, as it is written, where the children of Israel dwelt, there there was light; so, often, when a cloud covered the whole earth, bringing on a darkness that might be felt, a light shone around himself, the place, and the inhabitants thereof, where the saint was preaching. Rightly, therefore, as we believe, never were wet with any drops the garments of this saint, whose members he strove with the utmost care to preserve clean and pure from all defilement of flesh and blood. With justice also did a light shine forth from the darkness in the place of his preaching where he taught the people, as in his heart the Sun of Righteousness, the Light that knoweth no setting, ever shone; and he himself, like a lamp in a dark place, gave forth light in the midst of a perverse and wicked generation, as the apostle Peter beareth witness.

CHAPTER XXXVI.

*How the Saint miraculously restored to the Queen the Ring which
she had improperly given away, and which was thrown by
the King himself into the River Clud.*

So S. Kentigern having, as we have told, returned home, and
disposing himself to dwell by himself in mental solitude far
from the throngs of men, willed not to be freely seen in public
or to go abroad except in cases of great urgency. Nevertheless
he ceased not, though against his will, to shine forth abroad in
wondrous signs. Queen Languoreth, who has been mentioned
above, living in plenty and delights, was not faithful to the
royal chamber or the marital bed, as she ought to have been:
for the heap of her treasures, the exuberance of her means of
sensuality, and the elevation of power, were wont to minister
incentives and fuel to the will of the flesh. She cast her eyes
on a certain youth, a soldier, who, according to the perishing
beauty of this perishing flesh, seemed to her to be beautiful
and fair of aspect beyond many that were with him at court.
And he, who without external temptation was himself ready
enough for such a service as this, was easily induced to sin
with her.

So as time passed, and the forbidden pleasures, frequently
repeated, became more and more delightful to both of them—for
bread eaten in secret, and stolen waters, according to Solomon,
seemed to them to be sweeter; so from a rash act they proceeded to a blind love, and a royal ring of gold, set with a
precious gem, which her lawful husband had intrusted to her
as a special mark of his conjugal love, she very impudently and
imprudently bestowed upon her lover, and he, more impudently
and more imprudently placing it upon his finger, opened the
door of suspicion to all who were conversant in the matter. A
faithful servant of the king, finding this out, took care to
instil the secret of the queen and the soldier into the ears of
the husband, who did not willingly lend his ear or his mind to
her disgrace, as the unworthiness of his wife was brought to
him. It is an old and true proverb, It is difficult for a cuck-
old to put faith in one that reveals the failings of a beloved
wife; and the odium is apt to fall rather upon the informer
than upon the accused. But the detector of the adultery, in
proof of the matter, showed the ring on the finger of the soldier;

and by this proof persuading the king to believe him, he succeeded in kindling the spirit of jealousy within him.

So the king, being secretly assured of this, veiled under a calm demeanour the wrath of his soul against the queen and the soldier, and appeared more than usually cheerful and kind. But when a bright day occurred, he went out hunting, and summoning the soldier to accompany him, sought the woods and forests with a great company of beaters and dogs. Having uncoupled the dogs and stationed his friends at different places, the king with the soldier came down to the banks of the river Clud, and they, in a shady place on the green turf, thought it would be pleasant for both to sleep for a little. The soldier, worn out, and suspecting no danger, resting his head, stretching out his arm, and extending his hand, straightway slumbered; but the spirit of jealousy exciting the king, who simulated sleep, suffered him neither to slumber nor to take any rest. Seeing the ring on the finger of the sleeper, his wrath was kindled, and he with difficulty restrained his hand from his sword and from shedding of blood; but he controlled his rage, at least in part, and after drawing the ring off the finger threw it into the neighbouring river, and then, waking him up, ordered him to return to his companions and go home. The soldier waking up from sleep, and thinking nothing about the ring, obeyed the king's order, and never discovered what he had lost till he entered his house.

But when, on the return of the king, the queen in the usual manner came forth from her chamber and saluted him, from the mouth of him who was thus saluted there proceeded continuously threats, contempt, and reproach, while with flashing eyes and menacing countenance he demanded where the ring was which he had intrusted to her keeping. When she declared that she had it laid up in a casket, the king, in the presence of all his courtiers, commanded her to bring it to him with all haste; but she, still full of hope, entered the inner chamber as if to seek the ring, but straightway sent a messenger to the soldier, telling him of the anger of the king in demanding the ring, and ordering him to send it quickly. The soldier sent back to the queen to say that he had lost the ring and could not tell where. Then, fearing the face of the king, for the sake of concealment, he absented himself from court. In the meantime, as she sought further delays, and was slow in producing what, of course, she could not find, uselessly seeking here and there, the king in fury frequently calling her an adulteress, broke forth in curses saying, "God do to me, and more also, if I judge thee not according to the law of adulterers, and condemn thee to a

most disgraceful death. Thou, clinging to a young adulterer,
hast neglected the king thy spouse; yet I would have made
thee the sharer of my bed and the mistress of my kingdom:
thou hast done it in secret; I will do it in public, and the sun
shall manifest thine ignominy and reveal thy more shameful
things before thy face."

And when he had said much after this sort, all the courtiers
praying for some delay, he with difficulty conceded three days,
and ordered her to be imprisoned. Cast into a dungeon, she
now contemplated death as imminent; but not the less did her
guilty conscience torment her. O weighty and intolerable
punishment, the damning testimony of a guilty conscience!
Although one condemned to punishment may have external
peace, yet he is acknowledged to be wretched and disturbed
whom a gnawing conscience ceaselessly persecuteth. The spirit,
therefore, of the guilty woman was vexed within her, and with
contrite and lowly heart, with tearful prayer, she besought God
not to enter into judgment with His handmaiden, but according
to His great mercy, as formerly He had pity on the woman
taken in adultery and placed in the midst before Him, so in a
like case He would have mercy upon her. By the inspiration
of the Lord, the woman in her great strait found out a wise
device, and, sending a most faithful messenger to S. Kentigern,
told him her whole misfortune, and from him, as her only
deliverer, she urgently requested help. She also begged that
at least he would use his influence with the king and beseech
pardon for her, for there was nothing so great which he would,
or could, or ought to deny him.

The saintly bishop, instructed by the Holy Ghost and by
virtue from on high, knowing the whole story in order before
the arrival of the messenger, ordered him to go with a hook to
the bank of the river Clud aforesaid, to cast the hook into the
stream, and to bring back to him straightway the first fish that
was caught upon it and taken out of the water. The man did
what the saint commanded, and exhibited in the presence of
the man of God a large fish which is commonly called a
salmon; and on his ordering it to be cut open and gutted in
his presence, he found in it the ring in question, which he
straightway sent by the same messenger to the queen. And
when she saw it and received it, her heart was filled with joy,
her mouth with praise and thanksgiving; her grief was turned
into joy; the expectation of death into the dance of exultation
and safety. Therefore the queen rushed into the midst and
returned to the king the ring he had required, in the sight of
all. Wherefore the king and all his court were sorry for the

injuries done to the queen; and humbly on his knees he sought her pardon, and swore that he would inflict a very severe punishment, even death or exile if she willed, upon her slanderers. But she, wisely judging that mercy rather than the award of judgment was what she had to do with, was desirous that he should shew mercy, as a servant ought to have on his fellow-servant. She said, "Far be it, my lord, O King, that any one should suffer on my account; but if thou willest that from my heart I should forgive thee for what injury thou hast done me, I will that thou put away all angry feeling from thy heart and mind, as I do against mine accuser." And all, when they heard this, wondered and were glad. And so the king, and the queen, and the accuser are recalled to the grace of peace and mutual love. The queen, as soon as she could, betook herself to the man of God, and confessing her guilt, and making satisfaction by his advice, carefully corrected her life for the future and kept her feet from a similar fall. During her husband's lifetime she never revealed to any one the sign whereby the Lord had shown forth His mercy toward her, but after his death she told it to all who wished to know it.

Behold the Lord sitting in heaven willed to do by His servant Kentigern that which, clothed in our flesh, He condescended to do when conversing with men on earth. At His order Peter, casting a hook into the sea, drew out the great fish in whose mouth he found the piece of money, which he gave in tribute for the Lord and for himself. So by the command of S. Kentigern, in the Name of the Lord Jesus Christ, the queen's messenger, casting a hook into the river, took a fish, and bringing it thus to the saint found in it, when taken and opened, a ring which saved the queen from a double death. In both these cases, as it seemeth to me, there was rendered to Cæsar that which belongeth unto Cæsar, and unto God that which is God's. For in the piece of money the image of Cæsar was restored to him, and in the ring restored the flesh was redeemed from destruction, and the soul made in the image of God was cleansed from sin and restored to Him.

CHAPTER XXXVII.

How a Jester despising the gifts of the King demanded a dishful of fresh mulberries after Christmas; and how he received them through the instrumentality of S. Kentigern.

KING REDERECH was magnified by the Lord because he clung to Him, by serving Him in faith and good works, and because he obeyed the will of S. Kentigern. For glory and riches were in his house, generosity in his heart, politeness in his mouth, munificence in his hand, for that the Lord had blessed the works of his hands, so that not only to the regions in his own neighbourhood, but even across the sea to Ireland, the fame of his liberality extended. Wherefore a jester from one of the kings of Ireland, skilled and clever in his art, was sent to Cambria to the court of the king aforesaid, that he might see whether the truth responded to the fame of him, which was far and wide extended. The jester, admitted into the court, played with his hand on the timbrel and harp, and gave joy to the king and his paladins all the days of the Christmas holidays. When the feast of the Lord's holy epiphany was past, the king ordered gifts to be brought forth and bestowed upon the jester, in accordance with the royal generosity, all of which the actor refused, stating that he had sufficiency of such things in his own country. Being asked by the king what he would be willing to receive, he answered that he had no need whatsoever of silver, and gold, and garments, and horses, in which Ireland abounded; but "if thou desirest," said he, "that I should depart from thee well rewarded, let there be given to me a dish full of fresh mulberries." When they heard this speech uttered from the mouth of the man, all burst out laughing, because they thought that he was joking and speaking in sport; for a person of this kind is esteemed the more highly the better he is able, by words that produce mirth, to excite laughter. But he with an oath declared that he had demanded the mulberries not in jest but in all seriousness; nor could he be moved from this by prayers, promises, or the offer of the handsomest gifts; and rising, he declared that he wished to retire from the midst of the crowd, and, as the saying is, to carry off the king's honour. The king took this very ill, and asked his companions what could be done that he should not be dishonoured in this matter; for it was the season of winter and not a mulberry could be found anywhere. Acting on the advice of his courtiers, he betook himself to S. Kentigern, and humbly begged that by prayer he would obtain what he wanted from God. The man of God, although he thought that his prayer would not be fitly offered for such trifles as these, knew that the king had a great devotion to God and Holy Church, yet though his eyes beheld his substance, which was imperfect, in this case the holy bishop made up his mind to condescend to his petition, hoping that thereby in the future he might advance in virtue.   Therefore pondering for a time in his heart, and praying shortly, he said to the king, " Dost thou remember in what place during summer, thou didst throw away the garment with which thou wast girded, in the great heat when thou wast hunting, that thou mightest follow the dogs more expeditiously, and then forgetting or underrating it thou didst never return to recover what thou hadst cast off ?" The king answered, saying, " I know, my king and bishop, both the time and the place."   " Go," said the saint, "straightway to the place, and thou shalt find the garment still perfect, hanging over a bush of thorns, and below that thou shalt find mulberries sufficient still fresh and fit for gathering.   Take them and satisfy the demand of the jester, and in all things concern thyself that thou more and more reverence God, who will not allow thine honour to be marred or minished even in so light a thing as this."   The king did as the bishop ordered, and found all as he had predicted.   Therefore taking the dish and filling it with the mulberries, he gave it to the actor, saying, "There, take that which thou hast asked for; for by the help of the Lord who worketh with me, thou canst not in anything injure the fame of my generosity.   And that I may not seem to thee more niggardly than others, thou art welcome to stay here as long as it pleaseth thee."   The actor, seeing the charger full of mulberries contrary to the time of the year, wondered and feared, and when he knew how it had happened, he cried out and said, "Verily, there is none like unto thee among the kings of the earth, munificent in thy generosity, and there is none like unto Kentigern, glorious in holiness, fearful in praises, doing such wonders in my sight beyond expectation.   Henceforth I will not leave thy house or thy service, and I will be unto thee a servant for ever, so long as I live."   The actor therefore abode in the king's court, and served him for many days as jester.   Afterwards, by the instigation of the fear of God, he set himself against his former profession, renounced the trade of actor, and entering the ways of a better life, gave himself up to the service of God.

CHAPTER XXXVIII.

Of the two vessels filled with Milk which S. Kentigern sent to a certain workman; how, when the Milk was poured into the river, it became Cheese.

THERE was a certain man, skilled in the trade of an artisan, who served by hammering and forging, took charge of the

works of the man of God, and of the monastery, and received
from the saint the necessary wages. Now the saint was wont
to use milk as food and drink, for, as we have said above, he
usually abstained from all liquor that could intoxicate. He
therefore ordered vessels of new milk to be carried to the
artisan, because he knew that workmen and hired servants are
gratified by partaking of the food prepared for the lord and
householder. But when he who bore it was crossing the Clud,
the covers of the vessels, by the merest accident, became open,
and the whole milk was poured into the water. But, strangely
and wonderfully, the milk poured out did not mix with the
water, and was not altered as to colour and taste, but all at
once it became curded, and was turned into cheese. In fact,
that cheese was no less properly made solid by the beating
of the waves, than in other cases it is compacted by the pres-
sure of the hands. The bearer snatched the little shape of
cheese out of the water, and went and detailed from the beginning the whole story to the workman to whom the saint had
sent him. Many beheld this remarkable sign, and on seeing
that the fluid had not been turned into fluid, or liquefied, stood
astonished. But the workman and many others tasted of that
cheese, and also distributed minute particles piece by piece of
the same to many to be kept as relics. These relics are preserved
in many places and during many times, and making the beloved
and famous miracles of Kentigern more beloved and more
famous by the testimony of this very fact. But although this
sign, even externally, is the cause of great wonder, yet to those
who view it subtilly, and who infer spiritual from corporeal
things, the invisible things from the visible, it affords much
instruction. In the milk which fell into the waters, yet was
not mixed with them, nor turned into them, or immersed in
them, we have the example of preserving innocency and justice,
which are relics to a peaceable man, among those who swell
with pride, who would invade us with all evil, who dissipate
themselves in pleasures, and who seek to drown us in destruction by bad examples and persuasions. That the milk in the
stream was hardened into cheese, gives us an ensample of
maintaining constancy in the presence of trials and straits.
For the just and innocent man hardeneth among the waves, as
the milk did into cheese, when, in obedience to words proceeding from the mouth of God, he keepeth the hard paths, and
by many tribulations seeketh to enter into His kingdom. Moreover, if he endure threats, insults, losses, and injuries, from
wicked and froward men, then he feeleth them as though he did
not feel, but in peace possessing his soul, he endeavoureth to

persevere in good, knowing certainly that whosoever persevereth unto the end the same shall be saved.

CHAPTER XXXIX.

How S. Columba visited blessed Kentigern, and beheld a crown that came down from Heaven upon his head, and a celestial light shining around him.

AT the time when blessed Kentigern, placed in the Lord's candlestick, like a burning lamp, in ardent desires, and shining forth in lifegiving words, in the examples of virtues and miracles, gave light to all that were in the house of God, S. Columba, the abbot, whom the Angles call Columkillus, a man wonderful for doctrine and virtues, celebrated for his presage of future events, full of the spirit of prophecy, and living in that glorious monastery which he had erected in the Island of Yi, desired earnestly, not once and away, but continually to rejoice in the light of S. Kentigern. For hearing for a long time of the fame in which he was estimated, he desired to approach him, to visit him, to behold him, to come into his close intimacy, and to consult the sanctuary of his holy breast regarding the things which lay near his own heart. And when the proper time came the holy father S. Columba went forth, and a great company of his disciples, and of others who desired to behold and look upon the face of so great a man, accompanied him. When he approached the place called Mellindenor, where the saint abode at that time, he divided all his people into three bands, and sent forward a message to announce to the holy prelate his own arrival, and that of those who accompanied him.

The holy pontiff was glad when they said unto him these things concerning them, and calling together his clergy and people similarly in three bands, he went forth with spiritual songs to meet them. In the forefront of the procession were placed the juniors in order of time; in the second those more advanced in years; in the third, with himself, walked the aged in length of days, white and hoary, venerable in countenance, gesture, and bearing, yea, even in grey hairs. And all sang, " In the ways of the Lord how great is the glory of the Lord;" and again they answered, " The way of the just is made straight, and the path of the saints prepared." On S. Columba's side they sang with tuneful voices, "The saints shall go from strength to strength, until unto the God of gods appeareth every one in Sion," with the Alleluia. Meanwhile, some who had come with S. Columba asked him, saying, "Hath S. Kentigern come in the first chorus of singers?" The saint answered, " Neither in the first nor in the second cometh the gentle saint." And when they loudly asked how he knew this, he said, "I see a fiery pillar in fashion as of a golden crown, set with sparkling gems, descending from heaven upon his head, and a light of heavenly brightness encircling him like a certain veil, and covering him, and again returning to the skies. Wherefore it is given to me to know by this sign that, like Aaron, he is the elect of God, and sanctified; who, clothed with light as with a garment, and with a golden crown represented on his head, appeareth to me with the sign of sanctity." When these two godlike men met, they mutually embraced and kissed each other, and having first satiated themselves with the spiritual banquet of Divine words, they after that refreshed themselves with bodily food. But how great was the sweetness of Divine contemplation within these holy hearts is not for me to say, nor is it given to me, or to such as I am, to reveal the manna which is hidden, and, as I think, entirely unknown save unto them that taste it.

CHAPTER XL.

Of the head of S. Kentigern's ram, that was cut off, and how it was turned into stone.

WHILE these two men whom we have mentioned were mutually associated as two columns in the courts of the Lord's house, firmly founded in faith and love, and strengthened in the same, by the imitation and instruction of whom many peoples and tribes and tongues entered, and are still entering, into the heavenly temple, which is the joy of the Lord their God, some sons of the stranger, who had come with S. Columba, were confirmed in bad habits, and halted in the paths of the man of God. For as the Ethiopian cannot change his skin, so the man that is bred to theft and robbery findeth it difficult to change his malice. There came, therefore, some with the blessed Columba, who had no dovelike innocence, merely by the advances of their feet, and not by the affection of devotion, or by progress in morals. While they journeyed, they beheld from a distance one of the flocks of the holy bishop feeding, and leaving the path and going through dark ways, as it is said of such in the Proverbs, they turned aside thither, and, in spite of the struggles and remonstrances of the shepherds, seized the fattest wether. But the herdsman, in the Name of the Holy Trinity, and by the authority of S. Kentigern, forbade them to commit such robbery, nay, such sacrilege, on the flock of the holy bishop, informing them, that if they would but ask a ram of the saint, they would be sure to obtain it. But one of them insulted and drove away the shepherd, threatening him with some injury, or even with death, and carried away a ram, while the other, taking a knife, cut off its head. Then they took counsel how to carry off the carcase, and at a time and place that suited their crime, to skin it, so as they well knew how, to fit it more carefully for their use.

But a thing wonderful to relate, more wonderful to behold, took place. The ram with his head cut off rushed back with unaccountable speed to his flock, and there fell down; while the head, turned into stone, stuck firmly, as by some most cohesive glue, in the hands of him who held it and had struck it. They who were able to pursue, catch, hold, behead the ram living and strong, were unable to overtake it by following or pursuing when it was mutilated; nor could they cast away from their hands the head which had become stone, in spite of all their efforts. The men became rigid, and their hearts died within them, and became as stone, as they were carrying a stone, and at length they took the wise determination of betaking themselves to the saints, and, prostrate before the feet of S. Kentigern, penitent and confounded, they prayed with tears that he would pardon them. But the holy prelate, chiding them with kindly reproof, and warning them never again to commit fraud, theft, robbery, or, what was more detestable, sacrilege, unloosed them from the double bond, that of sin, and of the grasp of the stone. He ordered the carcase of the slain ram to be given them, and allowed them to depart. But the head turned into stone remaineth there unto this day, as a witness to the miracle, and, being mute, yet preacheth the merit of holy Kentigern.

Assuredly this miracle, as it seemeth to me, in the main, is not inferior to that which the book of Genesis records to have been wrought in the case of Lot's wife. When the heavenly fire, the avenger of the injury done to God, being ordered to destroy the wicked ones who would upset the natural laws of the generation of man, was about to descend, Lot, warned by the angelic counsel, and aided by its help, escaped the fire of

the overthrown and overwhelmed city of Sodom.　But his
wife, looking back in opposition to a command sent from
heaven, was turned into a rock, into an image of salt, to be a
relish to the food of brute animals.　Here the head of the ram
is turned into stone to condemn the hardness and cruelty of
those who carry off their neighbour's goods.　In the figure of
Lot's wife, by the Lord's own teaching, every faithful man is
taught and warned, not foolishly to turn back from any sacred
duty once undertaken.　In the head turned into stone, every
Christian is warned not to commit theft or fraud or rapine, or
any violence on the property of the Church or on the substance
of the servants of God.　In the very place, where the miracle
wrought by S. Kentigern came to the knowledge of S. Columba
and many others, there they interchanged their pastoral staves,
in pledge and testimony of their mutual love in Christ.　But
the staff which S. Columba gave to the holy bishop Kentigern
was preserved for a long time in the Church of S. Wilfred,
bishop and confessor at Ripun ; and held in great reverence on
account of the sanctity both of him who gave it and of him
who received it.　Wherefore, during several days, these saints,
passing the time together, mutually conversed on the things of
God and what concerned the salvation of souls ; then saying
farewell, with mutual love, they returned to their homes, never
to meet again.

CHAPTER XLI.

*How that the man of God erected Crosses in many places, by
which, even to the present day, miracles are wrought.*

THE venerable father and bishop Kentigern had a custom, in
the places in which at any time by preaching he had won the
people to the dominion of Christ, or had imbued them with the
faith of the cross of Christ, or had dwelt for any length of time,
there to erect the triumphant standard of the cross, that all
men might learn that he was in no ways ashamed of the cross of
our Lord Jesus Christ, which he carried on his forehead.　But, as
it seemeth unto me, this holy custom of the good man is in many
ways supported by sound reason.　For for this cause the saint
was accustomed to erect this lifegiving, holy, and terrible sign,
that, like as wax melteth at the fire, so the enemies of the
human race, the powers of the darkness of this world, melting away in terror before this sign, might disappear and in
terror and confusion might be banished far away.　Moreover,
it is fitting that the soldiers of the Eternal King, recognising

by a glance the unconquerable standard of their Chief, should fly to it, as to a tower of strength, from the face of the enemy, and from the face of those wicked ones who afflict them; and that they should have before their eyes that which they adore and in which they glory. And inasmuch as, according to the apostle, the wrestling against spiritual wickednesses in high places, and against the fiery darts of the evil one, is continual, it is meet and healthful that they should fortify and protect themselves by signing themselves with this sign; and by imitating the Passion of Christ, and with the apostle bearing about in their bodies the stigmata of the wounds of Christ, they should, for the love of the Crucified One, crucify the flesh with its vices and lusts, and the world to them, and themselves unto the world.

Therefore, among many crosses which he erected in several places where the word of the Lord was preached, he erected two which to the present time work miracles. One in his own city of Glasgu he caused to be cut by quarriers from a block of stone of wondrous size, which, by the united exertions of many men, and by the application of machinery, he ordered to be erected in the cemetery of the church of the Holy Trinity, in which his episcopal chair was placed. But all their labour was expended in vain; every machine was powerless, human strength and might availed not to raise it up, though much and long they toiled. But when human genius and help failed, the saint had recourse to the Divine aid. For on the succeeding night, which happened to be Sunday, and while the servant of the Lord was pouring forth his prayers for this end, an angel of the Lord descended from heaven, and coming near, rolled back the stone cross and raised it to the place where it standeth to-day, and blessing it with the sign of the cross, he signed it, sanctified it, and disappeared. The people, when they came to the church in the morning and saw what was done, were astonished and gave glory to God in His saint. For the cross was very large, and never from that time lacked great virtue, seeing that many maniacs and those vexed with unclean spirits are used to be tied of a Sunday night to that cross, and in the morning they are found restored, freed, and cleansed, though ofttimes they are found dead or at the point of death.

He constructed another cross, wonderful to be described, unless it could be tested by sight and touch, of simple sea-sand, in Lothwerverd, while he meditated righteously and religiously of the Resurrection. In this place he abode eight years. Who ought to dispute on this truth, and say that the Lord will not raise our mortal bodies though turned into dust, since He hath so promised with His blessed mouth, when in His name, this saint, of like passions with ourselves, by praying to God raised up a cross formed of sea-sand? Verily it must be believed that at the Lord's will all the bones of the dead shall be joined to their bones, according to the prophecy of Ezechiel, and that the Lord will give them sinews and make flesh to come on them, and skin to cover them, and shall put breath into them, and they shall live for ever; seeing that at the prayer of a man still alive, a collection of the minutest sand, I had almost said of atoms, was extended into a solid and perfect matter, a mass of sand was condensed and formed into a cross, which neither the burning sun by day, nor the frost by night, nor any inclemency of the atmosphere can dissolve. That cross then was formed as proof to our faith that this our corruptible must put on incorruption; and that of the multitude of the children of Israel, if they were as the sand of the sea, a remnant shall be saved by the faith of the cross of Christ; and that the friends of God shall be multiplied beyond the number of the sand by Him who numbereth the stars of heaven, and the sand of the sea, and the drops of rain, and the days of the age. To this cross also many afflicted with divers diseases, and specially madmen and those vexed by the devil, are bound in the evening; and ofttimes in the morning they are found safe and sound, and return to their friends.

There are many other places in which he lived, specially during Lent, unknown to us, which the saint sanctified by the presence of His holy indwelling. Yet very many persons relate numerous instances regarding those which, by sure tokens to this day, diffuse the odour of his sanctity, and by his merits afford many blessings to the feeble, and possess the efficacy of miracles.

CHAPTER XLII.

How he tied up his Chin with a certain bandage, and how he prepared for his Soul's Departure.

BLESSED Kentigern, overcome by excessive old age, perceived from many cracks in it that the ruin of his earthly house was imminent; but the foundation of his faith, which was founded on the Rock, comforted his soul; for he trusted that when the earthly house of this tabernacle was dissolved, he had prepared for him a house not made with hands, eternal in the heavens. And because by reason of the extremity of old age, and the infirmity consequent thereon, the fastenings of his nerves were almost entirely withered throughout his body and loosened, therefore he bound up his cheeks and his chin, by a certain linen bandage, which went over his head and under his chin, neither too tight nor too loose. This the most refined man did, that by the fall of his chin nothing indecent should appear in the gaping of his mouth, and that such a support should render him more ready in bringing forth what he could or would.

In the end, this man, beloved by God and man, knowing that the hour was drawing near when he should pass out of this world to the Father of lights, fortified himself with the sacred unction which wrought remission of sin, and with the life-giving sacraments of the Lord's Body and Blood, in order that the ancient serpent, seeking to bruise his heel, should be unable to fix thereon his poisonous tooth or to inflict on him a deadly wound: yea rather, that with bruised head he should retreat in confusion. In this very way, the Lord treading Satan under his feet, in order that his holy soul should not be speedily put to confusion, when in his coming out of Egypt he spake with his enemies in the gate, he patiently, like an excellent under-pilot, awaited the Lord, who had saved him from the storms of this world. And now, close to the shore, driven into the harbour of a certain inward quietude, after so many dangers of the sea, he cast out the anchor of hope, with the ropes of his desire well bound, in the solid and soft ground, reaching of a truth even to the inside of the veil, whither Jesus Christ had gone before him. Henceforward he alone awaited the departure from the tents of Kedar and the entrance into the land of the living, so that in the City of Powers, that is the heavenly Jerusalem, like a successful wrestler he might receive from the hand of the heavenly King the crown of glory and the diadem of the kingdom which shall not be destroyed. He warned his disciples, gathered around him, so far as his strength would allow him, concerning the observance of the holy rule, the maintenance of love and peace, of the grace of hospitality, and of the continuing instant in prayer and holy study. But above all things he gave them short but peremptory commands, warning them to avoid every evil appearance of simoniacal wickedness, and to shun entirely the communion and society of heretics and schismatics, and observe strictly the decrees of the holy fathers, and especially the laws and customs of Holy Church, the mother of all. After that, as was right, he gave to each of them, as they humbly knelt before him, the kiss of peace; and lifting his hand as best he could, he blessed them, and bidding them his last farewell, he committed them all to the guardianship of the Holy Trinity, and to the protection of the holy Mother of God, and gathered himself up into his stone bed. Then one voice of mourners sounded full everywhere, and a horror of confusion fell on the faces of all of them.

CHAPTER XLIII.

Of his Disciples, who sought a speedy journey to heaven, and of his warm bath.

SOME of them, who very dearly loved the saint of God, prostrating themselves in tears before him, besought him thus: "We find, O Lord Bishop, that thou desirest to depart and to be with Christ. For thine old age, venerable, long protracted, and measured by many years, as well as thy spotless life, demand this; but, we pray thee, have mercy upon us whom thou hast begotten in Christ. For wheresoever we have erred through human frailty we have always confessed in thy presence, and by satisfaction have made amends by the judgment of thy discretion. Since then we have no power of retaining thee longer among us, pray to the Lord that it may be vouchsafed to us to depart with thee from this vale of tears to the glory of thy Lord. So far as concerns this we believe in truth and assert that the Divine mercy will grant thee what thou askest, for the will of God hath been to us directed in thy hand from thy youth upwards. It seemeth to us improper that the bishop without his clergy, the shepherd without any of his flock, the father without his children, should enter into these joyous and festive abodes; yea rather, the more festive and the more sublime, by how much a greater company of his own should attend him." And when they had urged him more with tears, the man of God, full of compassion, collecting his breath, as best he might, said, "The will of the Lord be done in us all: and do with us as He best knoweth, and as is well-pleasing unto Him."

After these things the saint was silent, and sighing in his soul for heaven, he awaited the passage of his spirit from the body; and his disciples watching by him, took care of him as if close to death. And behold, while the morning day-star, the messenger of the dawn, the herald of the light of day, tearing in sunder the pall of the darkness of night, shone forth with flaming rays, an angel of the Lord appeared with unspeakable splendour, and the glory of God shone around him. And for fear of him the guardians of the holy bishop were exceedingly astonished and amazed, being but earthly vessels, and, unable to bear the weight of so great glory, became as dead men. But the holy old man, comforted by the vision and visit of the angel, and, as it were, forgetting his age and infirmity, being made strong, experienced some foretastes of the blessedness now near at hand, and held close converse with the angel as with his closest and dearest friend.

Now the heavenly messenger said these words to him:— " Kentigern, chosen and beloved of God, rejoice and be glad, let thy soul magnify the Lord, for He hath greatly increased His mercy towards thee. Thy prayer is heard, and the Divine ear hath listened to the preparation of thy heart. It shall be to thy disciples who desire to accompany thee as thou willest. Therefore be ye steadfast, and ye shall see the help of the Lord toward you. To-morrow ye shall go forth from the body of this death into the unfailing life; and the Lord shall be with you, and ye shall be with Him for ever. And because thy whole life in this world hath been a continual martyrdom, it hath pleased the Lord that thy mode of leaving it shall be easier than that of other men. Cause, therefore, on the morrow that a warm bath be prepared for thee, and entering therein, thou shalt fall asleep in the Lord without pain, and take thy quiet rest in Him. And after that thou hast paid the debt to nature, and even before the water hath begun to cool but is yet warm about thee, let thy brethren follow thee into the bath, and straightway, loosed from the bonds of death, they shall migrate with thee as companions of thy journey, and being introduced into the splendours of the saints, they shall with thee enter into the joy of the Lord."

With these words the angelic vision and voice departed; but a fragrance of wondrous and unspeakable odour in a strange way filled the place and all that were therein. And the holy man, calling together his disciples, revealed to them in due order the secret of the angel, and ordered that his bath should be prepared as the Lord commanded by his messenger; and his brethren above mentioned rendered unmeasured thanks to God Almighty and to their holy father Kentigern, and thus assured by the oracle in every way they could, fortified by the Divine Sacraments, prepared themselves for what was awaiting them.

CHAPTER XLIV.

How he passed out of this world, and how he shone forth after his death in many Miracles.

WHEN the octave of the Lord's Epiphany, on which the gentle bishop himself had been wont every year to wash a multitude of people in sacred baptism, was dawning,—a day very acceptable to S. Kentigern and to the spirits of the sons of his adoption,—the holy man, borne by their hands, entered a vessel filled with hot water, which he had first blessed with the sign of salvation; and a circle of the brethren standing round him, awaited the issue of the event. And when the saint had been some little time in it, after lifting his hands and his eyes to heaven, and bowing his head as if sinking into a calm sleep, he yielded up his spirit. For he seemed as free from the pain of death as he stood forth spotless and pure from the corruption of the flesh and the snares of this world.

The disciples, seeing what was taking place, lifted the holy body out of the bath, and eagerly strove with each other to enter the water; and so, one by one, before the water cooled, they slept in the Lord in great peace, and having tasted death along with their holy bishop, they entered with him into the mansions of heaven. And when the water cooled, not only the fear of death, but every spark of discomfort, wholly disappeared.

My judgment is that this bath is to be compared with the sheep-pool of Bethesda, in which, after the descent of the angel and the troubling of the water, one sick man was healed of whatsoever infirmity he had, but he was still liable to death. But in this ablution a very great company of saints is set free from all sickness, to live for ever with Christ. The water of that laver was distributed to divers persons in divers places; and from its being drunk or sprinkled health was conferred upon many sick persons in various ways.

The brethren stripped the saint of his ordinary clothes, which they partly reserved and partly distributed as precious relics, and clothed him in the consecrated garments which became so great a bishop. Then he was carried by the brethren into the choir with chants and psalms, and the life-giving Victim was offered to God for him by many. Diligently and most devoutly, as the custom of the Church in those days demanded, celebrated they his funeral; and on the right side of the altar laid they beneath a stone, with as much becoming reverence as they could, that abode of virtues, that precious stone, by whose merit, as it was a time for collecting stones for the building of the heavenly edifice of the temple, many elect and living stones, along with that pearl, were taken up and laid in the treasures of the Great King. The sacred remains of all these brethren were devoutly and disposedly consigned to the cemetery for sepulture, in the order in which they had followed the holy bishop out of this life.

Thus blessed Kentigern, full of years, when he was one hundred and eighty-five years old, matured in merit, famous for signs, wonders and prophecies, left this world and went to the Father on this wise :—from faith to sight; from labour to rest; from exile to fatherland; from the course to the crown; from the present misery to eternal glory. Blessed, I say, is that man to whom the heavens were opened, who penetrated the sanctuary and entered into the powers of the Lord, received by the angel hosts; marshalled among the hosts of patriarchs and prophets; joined to the choirs of the apostles; mixed up in the ranks of those martyrs who are crowned by the purple of their rosy blood; associated with the sacred confessors of the Lord; crowned with the snow-white choirs of virgins. And no wonder; for he was indeed, in office and desert, an angel of the Lord, who announced to those who were far away, and those who were near, peace and safety in the Blood of Christ; whose lips kept true wisdom; at whose mouth very many people sought and found the law of God. He, moreover, was a prophet of the Most High, who knew many things in absence, foresaw and predicted many things that were to come to pass. For he rightly is called, and is, the Apostle of the region of Cambria, since its inhabitants and many other people are the signs of his apostleship. He deservedly is called martyr, who by constant and uninterrupted martyrdom mortified himself for Christ, and was proved to have had his heart prepared to sustain any kind of death, should the occasion require it. For, for the name of Christ, and for the defence of truth and righteousness, he frequently offered himself to persecution, proscription, the wiles and swords of the enemies of the cross of Christ; and truly and happily triumphed over the flesh, the world, the devil and his satellites. He, by change of terms, is called the Confessor of Christ, who, confessing the Name of Christ before Gentiles and kings, preached with courage, and instigated all men to the profession of the Name of Christ, and to the confession of their own sins, and of the Christian Faith and praise of God. Nevertheless he by special prerogative obtained the glory and honour of virgins, because from the tamarisk he extracted the balsam, from the nettle the lily, and while in the vessel of this frail and perishing body, he never disturbed, as they say, even by a look, his angelic celibacy, and preserved in a vessel of clay the heavenly treasure of chastity. Wherefore from a virgin body he soared in white to the white-robed company of the virgins, that without stain he might stand by the Throne of God and of the Lamb, and following Him whithersoever He goeth, might sing the new song which was only known to those who had not defiled their garments. Justly, therefore, the holy man liveth as the companion, fellow-citizen, and partaker with all the saints, seeing that in this life he had communion with them, and always sought to please, obey, cling to, and be united in spirit to the Saint of Saints, the Sanctifier of all; and now and ever, being united to them with Him, he liveth and rejoiceth.

The spirit of S. Kentigern being taken up to the starry realms, that which the Earth, the mother of all, had bestowed she gathered into her womb. But the power of miracles which had existed in him when alive could not be hid behind the turf or stone, but burst forth. From the very day of his burial to the present time his sacred bones are known to put forth power from their own place, and do not cease to announce, by benefits bestowed on many kinds of witnesses, that both in heaven and earth the righteous is had in everlasting remembrance. At his tomb sight is restored to the blind, hearing to the deaf, the power of walking to the lame, strength of limb to the paralytic, a sound mind to the insane, speech to the dumb, cleanness of skin to the lepers. Impious, sacrilegious, perjured men, the violators of the peace of the Church and the profaners of holy places, are justly punished.

For once upon a time a certain man by night stole away from Glasgu a cow, which in the morning was found living and bound to the foot of the thief, who had been deprived of life; which excited both astonishment and joy. Many who, having committed sins of the flesh, had not hesitated to profane the sanctuary by their impure footsteps, were sometimes either cut off by sudden death, or mutilated in their limbs, or afflicted by some incurable and protracted disease. The breakers of his peace often suffered thus. Those who presumed, by any servile work, to dishonour the anniversary of the saint, on which at Glasgu, where his most sacred body resteth, a great multitude is used to assemble from all quarters to seek his intercession, and to behold the miracles which are wont to take place there, have often experienced in themselves a speedy vengeance.

CHAPTER XLV.

Of the Prophecy of a certain man, and of the Burial of the Saints in Glasgow.

In the same year that S. Kentigern, set free from earthly things, migrated to the heavens, King Rederech, who has been often mentioned before, remained much longer than usual in the royal town, which was called Pertnech. In his court there lived a fool called Laloecen, who was in the habit of receiving the necessaries of food and clothing from the munificence of the king; for the chiefs of the earth, the sons of the kingdom, given to vanity, are used to have such persons about them, that by their foolish words and gestures they may excite to jokes and loud laughter the lords themselves and their servants. This man, after the death of S. Kentigern, gave himself up to the most extreme grief, and would receive no consolation from any one.

When they asked him why he mourned so inconsolably, he answered that his lord, King Rederech, and another of the chiefs of the land, by name Morthec, would not live long after the death of the holy bishop, but would die within the year. That the saying of the fool was uttered not foolishly but prophetically, was clearly proved by the fact of the death of both in the same year. Nor is it much to be marvelled at that the Creator of all things should allow to be announced through the mouth of a fool what was determined, when even Balaam the soothsayer, by his inspiration seeing beforehand many important events, with foreboding mind declared them; and when Caiaphas prophesied that the redemption of the people was to come from the death of Christ; when by the mouth of a she-ass the madness of a prophet was rebuked; when the destruction of Jerusalem was foretold by a madman, as Josephus writes. Therefore in the same year in which the holy Bishop Kentigern died, the king and prince aforesaid died and were buried in Glasgu.

In the cemetery of the church of that city, as the inhabitants and countrymen assert, 665 saints rest; and all the great men of that region for a long time have been in the custom of being buried there. O how much is that place to be feared and had in reverence which so many pledges of the saints adorn as their resting-place! and which so precious a confessor decorateth with the sacred spoils of his mortality and adorneth with such frequent miracles, that if everything were written they would be found to fill many volumes.   Not only in the place where he resteth in the body, though there most frequently, and on his anniversary, is he used to shine forth in signs, but in almost all places, in the churches, and chapels, and altars where his memory is held in honour, he is present as a powerful helper in necessities to those who are placed in tribulations, to those who love him, and trust him, and call upon him.   And where faith or certain reason demandeth it, he doth not cease to shine forth in miracles, to the praise and glory of our Lord Jesus Christ; to whom is glory, praise, honour, and power, for ever and ever. Amen.

Here endeth the Life of the most holy Kentigern, Bishop and Confessor, who is also called Mungu.